County Council

Libraries, books and more . . .

Please return/renew this item by the last due date.
Library items may be renewed by phone on
030 33 33 1234 (24 hours) or via our website
www.cumbria.gov.uk/libraries

CLIC
Interactive Catalogue

Ask for a CLIC password

THE
NO SUGAR
RECIPE BOOK

DAVID GILLESPIE

PHOTOGRAPHY BY BEN DEARNLEY

MICHAEL JOSEPH
an imprint of
PENGUIN BOOKS

KFAST

PANCAKES WITH MASCARPONE

MAKES 8

115g self-raising flour, sifted

45g dextrose

2 eggs

185ml buttermilk

2 teaspoons vanilla essence,
   or to taste

butter, for pan-frying

mascarpone, blueberries (optional)
   and mint (optional), to serve

You can top these delicious fluffy pancakes with the
Strawberry and Rhubarb Jam on page 190 or rice malt
syrup instead of blueberries and mascarpone, if you prefer.

1   Mix the flour and dextrose in a bowl. Make a well in the centre.
    Add the eggs, buttermilk and vanilla and whisk until smooth.
    Set aside for 10 minutes.

2   Heat a little butter in a large non-stick frying pan over medium
    heat. Cook a small ladleful (about 2 tablespoons) of the mixture
    for each pancake for 2-3 minutes on each side or until golden
    and cooked through.

3   Serve the pancakes immediately with mascarpone, blueberries
    and mint, if you like.

- - - - - - - - - - - - - - - - - - - -

» VARIATION:

To make chocolate pancakes,
replace 35g of the flour with
35g cup cocoa powder.

RICOTTA & CINNAMON MUFFINS

MAKES 12

300g plain flour

3 teaspoons ground cinnamon, or to taste

2 teaspoons baking powder

170g dextrose

250g firm ricotta, drained

2 eggs

125ml milk

125ml olive oil

1 tablespoon finely grated orange zest

2 teaspoons vanilla essence, or to taste

» VARIATION:

To vary the flavour of these muffins add fruit such as blueberries, mashed banana or unpeeled chopped or grated apple or pear.

The addition of ricotta makes these moreish muffins light and moist.

1 Preheat the oven to 180°C (160°C fan-assisted). Lightly grease and line a 12-hole muffin tin with paper cases.

2 Sift the flour, cinnamon and baking powder into a medium bowl. Add the dextrose and stir to combine.

3 In a separate bowl, whisk the ricotta, eggs, milk, oil, orange zest and vanilla until combined. Fold the ricotta mixture through the flour mixture until just combined; don't over-mix or the muffins will be tough. Spoon the batter evenly into the paper cases.

4 Bake the muffins for 30–35 minutes or until cooked when tested with a skewer. Leave to cool in the tin for 5 minutes, then transfer to a wire rack to cool.

5 Store any leftover muffins wrapped individually in plastic film or freezer bags in an airtight container in the freezer for up to 1 month.

GRANOLA BARS

MAKES 10

These are a terrific substitute for sugar-loaded purchased muesli bars.

270g rolled oats
45g shredded coconut
70g pumpkin seeds
30g sesame seeds
1 tablespoon ground cinnamon, or to taste
1 teaspoon vanilla essence, or to taste
360g glucose syrup
35g dextrose
80g unsalted butter, chopped

1   Preheat the oven to 170°C (150°C fan-assisted). Grease and line a 30cm × 20cm slice tin with baking paper.

2   Mix the oats, coconut, pumpkin seeds, sesame seeds and cinnamon in a large bowl until well combined.

3   Put the vanilla, glucose, dextrose and butter into a small saucepan. Bring to the boil, then reduce the heat to medium and simmer for 2-3 minutes. Pour over the oat mixture and mix until well combined. Spoon into the prepared tin.

4   Bake the oat mixture for 25-30 minutes or until golden. Leave to cool completely in the tin.

5   Remove from the tin, then trim the edges and cut into ten 10cm × 7cm bars. Wrap each bar in baking paper. Store in an airtight container in the fridge for up to 2 days.

CRUNCHY GRANOLA WITH YOGHURT ❯

MAKES ABOUT 8 BOWLS

You can add any nuts you like to this basic granola recipe – try walnuts, pecans, macadamias or almonds.

180g rice malt syrup
125ml olive oil
270g rolled oats
60g sunflower seeds
70g pumpkin seeds
1 tablespoon ground cinnamon, or to taste milk and natural live yoghurt, to serve

1   Preheat the oven to 180°C (160°C fan-assisted). Lightly grease a baking tray and line with baking paper.

2   Put the syrup and oil into a small saucepan and cook over low heat for 2 minutes, stirring until warmed through.

3   Mix the oats, sunflower seeds, pumpkin seeds and cinnamon in a bowl. Pour over the syrup mixture and stir to combine. Transfer the mixture to the prepared tray, spreading it out in an even layer.

4   Bake the granola for 20-25 minutes or until golden. Leave to cool on the tray. Serve with milk and yoghurt. Store in an airtight container for up to 7 days.

LEMON SCONES

MAKES 12

450g self-raising flour, sifted, plus extra for dusting

105g dextrose

1 tablespoon finely grated lemon zest

75g cold unsalted butter, chopped

315ml buttermilk

milk, for brushing

Roasted Strawberry & Rhubarb Jam (see page 190) (optional), to serve

Enjoy these tangy scones for breakfast with strawberry jam or natural yoghurt, which can be mixed with a drop of vanilla essence for extra flavour. They are also a great addition to the school lunch-box or for an after-school treat.

1 Preheat the oven to 180°C (160°C fan-assisted). Line a baking tray with baking paper.

2 Mix the flour, dextrose and lemon zest in a bowl to combine. Add the butter, then use your fingertips to rub it into the flour mixture until it resembles fine breadcrumbs. Make a well in the centre and pour in the buttermilk. Use a butter knife to gradually mix the buttermilk into the flour mixture until just combined.

3 Turn the dough out onto a lightly floured surface and gently bring it together. Roll out until 2cm thick, then use a 6cm round cutter to cut out 12 rounds. Put the scones onto the prepared tray and brush with milk.

4 Bake the scones for 18-20 minutes or until cooked when tested with a skewer.

5 Serve with strawberry jam, if you like. These are best eaten on the day they are made.

LITTLE COCONUT BREADS

MAKES 10

2 eggs
350ml coconut milk
2 teaspoons vanilla essence,
   or to taste
335g plain flour
2 teaspoons baking powder
205g dextrose
100g desiccated coconut
75g unsalted butter, melted
shredded coconut, for sprinkling

If you don't have mini loaf tins use a 21cm × 9cm loaf tin instead; just increase the cooking time to 45–50 minutes. You can then cut the loaf into slices, wrap them individually in plastic film and freeze until needed. I like these for breakfast, but they are also a welcome addition to school lunch-boxes or served for afternoon tea. Leftovers can be toasted and spread with butter.

1 Preheat the oven to 160°C (140°C fan-assisted). Lightly grease and line ten mini loaf tins.

2 Whisk the eggs, coconut milk and vanilla in a bowl.

3 Sift the flour and baking powder into a large bowl. Add the dextrose and coconut and stir to combine. Make a well in the centre, then add the egg mixture and butter and stir to combine. Spoon the batter evenly into the prepared tins and sprinkle with shredded coconut.

4 Bake the breads for 25-30 minutes or until cooked when tested with a skewer. Leave to cool in the tins for 5 minutes, then turn out onto a wire rack to cool completely. Store any leftovers individually wrapped in plastic film or freezer bags in an airtight container in the freezer for up to 1 month.

SPICED PUMPKIN MUFFINS

MAKES 6

225g plain flour
1 teaspoon baking powder
1 teaspoon ground cinnamon
1 teaspoon ground nutmeg
135g dextrose
250g cooled mashed pumpkin
100ml olive oil
2 eggs

These lightly spiced muffins are a great way to use up leftover cooked pumpkin and taste a little bit like pumpkin pie. If you prefer the taste of wholemeal flour then use it instead of plain flour. Simply double the quantities if you wish to make 12 muffins.

1 Preheat the oven to 180°C (160°C fan-assisted). Lightly grease and line 6 holes of a 12 hole-capacity muffin tin with paper cases or baking paper.

2 Sift the flour, baking powder, cinnamon and nutmeg into a large bowl. Add the dextrose and stir to combine well.

3 Put the pumpkin, oil and eggs into a large bowl and whisk until smooth. Fold the pumpkin mixture into the flour mixture until just combined; don't over-mix or the muffins will be tough. Spoon the batter evenly into the prepared paper cases.

4 Bake the muffins for 30-35 minutes or until cooked when tested with a skewer. Transfer to a wire rack to cool.

5 Store any leftover muffins individually wrapped in plastic film or freezer bags in an airtight container in the freezer for up to 1 month.

» VARIATION:
Scatter the batter with pumpkin seeds before baking for a little extra crunch.

COOKIE
BISC

ES &
UITS

DOUBLE CHOCOLATE CHIP COOKIES

MAKES 24

125g unsalted butter, chopped
  and softened

135g dextrose

1 teaspoon vanilla essence,
  or to taste

1 egg

125g plain flour, sifted

75g self-raising flour, sifted

40g cocoa powder, sifted

½ teaspoon bicarbonate of soda

40g Sugar-free Chocolate (see
  page 168), roughly chopped

To replicate an authentic chocolate chip experience, make your own chocolate chips with the sugar-free chocolate on page 168.

1   Preheat the oven to 170°C (150°C fan-assisted). Line 2 baking trays with baking paper.

2   Beat the butter, dextrose and vanilla with an electric mixer until light and creamy. Add the egg and beat until just combined. Add the plain flour, self-raising flour, cocoa and bicarbonate of soda and continue to beat until just combined. Stir through the chopped chocolate.

3   Roll tablespoons of the dough into 24 balls and put onto the prepared trays, leaving room for them to spread a little, then flatten slightly.

4   Bake the cookies for 10-12 minutes or until cooked. Leave to cool on the trays for 5 minutes, then transfer to a wire rack to cool completely. Store in an airtight container for up to 2 days.

CLASSIC SHORTBREAD

MAKES 8 WEDGES

250g cold unsalted
  butter, chopped

205g dextrose, plus extra
  for dusting (optional)

185g plain flour, sifted

75g rice flour, sifted

2 teaspoons vanilla essence,
  or to taste

While shortbread can be made with plain flour alone, adding rice flour produces a lighter result.

1 Preheat the oven to 170°C (150°C fan-assisted). Lightly grease a 22cm springform cake tin.

2 Process the butter, dextrose, plain flour, rice flour and vanilla in a food processor until the mixture just comes together to form a dough.

3 Lightly press the dough into the prepared tin, using the back of a spoon to smooth the top. Refrigerate for 15 minutes or until firm. Use a sharp knife to score the dough into 8 wedges and prick with a skewer.

4 Bake the shortbread for 40-50 minutes or until golden. Remove from the tin and leave to cool on a wire rack.

5 Cut into wedges and dust with extra dextrose, if desired, to serve. Store in an airtight container for up to 2 days.

- - - - - - - - - - - - - - - - - - - -

» VARIATION:

If you wish to use this shortbread recipe to make individual biscuits, simply roll out the dough until 5mm or so thick, then cut it into shapes with your choice of cookie cutter. It's the perfect base recipe for making holiday-themed cookies for Easter, Christmas or Halloween.

ANZAC BISCUITS

MAKES 18

150g wholemeal plain flour, sifted
90g rolled oats
90g desiccated coconut
70g dextrose
125g unsalted butter, chopped
120ml rice malt syrup
1 tablespoon water
1 teaspoon bicarbonate of soda

Wholemeal flour adds a slight nutty taste to these traditional biscuits, but you can substitute it with plain flour if that's what's in your pantry. These are best eaten on the day they are made as they will soften a little when stored.

1 Preheat the oven to 160°C (140°C fan-assisted). Line 2 baking trays with baking paper.

2 Mix the flour, oats, coconut and dextrose in a medium bowl.

3 Put the butter, syrup and water into a medium saucepan and bring just to the boil over medium heat. Whisk in the bicarbonate of soda and allow the mixture to foam up. Pour the butter mixture over the dry ingredients and stir until well combined.

4 Drop tablespoons of the mixture onto the prepared trays, leaving room between them for the mixture to spread.

5 Bake the biscuits for 20-25 minutes or until golden. Transfer to wire racks to cool completely. Store in an airtight container for up to 2 days.

- - - - - - - - - - - - - - - - - -

» VARIATION:

If you prefer a more cake-like texture, roll the mixture into balls, then only flatten them slightly before baking. For a crisper result, squash the dough flat before baking.

VANILLA STAR BISCUITS

MAKES 24

250g unsalted butter, chopped and softened

135g dextrose

1 egg yolk

2 teaspoons vanilla essence, or to taste

300g plain flour, sifted

This is a terrific basic cookie dough to have in your repertoire. The kids can cut the dough into any shape they like, then decorate the finished biscuits with the egg-white icing on page 192.

1   Beat the butter and dextrose with an electric mixer for 8–10 minutes or until light and creamy. Add the egg yolk and vanilla and beat to combine. Add the flour and beat until a smooth dough forms.

2   Wrap the dough in plastic film and refrigerate for 30 minutes.

3   Preheat the oven to 180°C (160°C fan-assisted). Line 2 baking trays with baking paper.

4   Roll out the dough between 2 sheets of baking paper until 5mm thick. Use a 9cm star-shaped cookie cutter to cut out cookies and place on the prepared baking trays.

5   Bake the biscuits for 10–12 minutes or until light golden. Leave to cool on the trays for 5 minutes, then transfer to wire racks to cool completely. Store in an airtight container for up to 2 days.

LEMON & PISTACHIO BISCOTTI

MAKES 24

3 egg whites
90g dextrose
75g plain flour, sifted
100g peeled pistachios, chopped
2 tablespoons finely grated
   lemon zest

These biscotti are not as hard and crisp as sugar-based biscotti – they are a little softer and more bread-like. Perfect to have with a cup of tea.

1 Preheat the oven to 160°C (140°C fan-assisted). Grease and line a 25cm × 7cm loaf tin.

2 Whisk the egg whites with an electric mixer until soft peaks form. With the motor running, gradually add the dextrose, whisking until stiff peaks form. Fold in the flour, pistachios and lemon zest until well combined. Spoon into the prepared loaf tin.

3 Bake the mixture for 35–40 minutes or until golden on top.

4 Remove from the tin, then leave on a wire rack to cool completely.

5 Increase the oven temperature to 180°C (160° fan-assisted). Line 2 baking trays with baking paper.

6 Cut the biscotti into 1cm-thick slices and put onto the prepared trays, cut-side down. Bake for 8–10 minutes or until just golden. Store in an airtight container for up to 2 days.

ORANGE & CHOCOLATE FLORENTINES

MAKES 46

375g dextrose
65ml glucose syrup
50g unsalted butter, chopped
65ml double cream
100g flaked almonds
2 tablespoons finely grated
  orange zest
100g plain flour, sifted
40g cocoa powder, sifted
125ml boiling water

Florentines are traditionally made with candied cherries, however, we have used orange zest here instead. When combined with the chocolate glaze, the result is a delicious jaffa-like flavour.

1   Preheat the oven to 160°C (140° fan-assisted). Line 2 baking trays with baking paper.

2   Put 105g of the dextrose and the glucose, butter and cream into a medium saucepan and stir over medium heat until melted and combined. Bring to the boil, then reduce the heat to low and simmer for 6–9 minutes or until the mixture has thickened.

3   Remove the pan from the heat, then stir through the almonds, orange zest and flour. Place teaspoons of the mixture onto the prepared trays, leaving space between for them to spread.

4   Bake the biscuits for 5–7 minutes or until lacy and golden. Leave to cool completely on the trays.

5   Put the cocoa, water and remaining 270g of the dextrose into a medium heatproof bowl over a saucepan of boiling water and stir until melted and well combined; make sure the bottom of the bowl does not touch the water.

6   Dip half of each cooled biscuit into the chocolate mixture, then transfer to a baking tray lined with baking paper to cool and set. Store in an airtight container for up to 2 days.

CHOCOLATE CARAMEL SANDWICH BISCUITS

MAKES 16 SANDWICHES (32 BISCUITS)

150g unsalted butter, chopped
and softened

90g dextrose

2 teaspoons vanilla essence,
or to taste

185g plain flour, sifted

2 tablespoons cocoa
powder, sifted

2 tablespoons cornflour, sifted

Caramel filling

135g dextrose

85g unsalted butter, chopped

125ml double cream

1 tablespoon cornflour

1 tablespoon water

The creamy caramel centre between these chocolaty biscuits will win over any sugarholic. You can use the caramel as a filling for a caramel tart made with the pastry on page 80.

1 Beat the butter, dextrose and vanilla with an electric mixer for 8-10 minutes or until light and creamy. Add the flour, cocoa and cornflour and beat until a dough forms. Form the dough into a disc, then wrap in plastic film and refrigerate for 30 minutes.

2 Preheat the oven to 180°C (160°C fan-assisted). Line 2 baking trays with baking paper.

3 Roll out the dough between 2 sheets of baking paper until 5mm thick. Use a 5cm cookie cutter to cut out rounds from the dough, placing them on the prepared trays as you go.

4 Bake the biscuits for 10-12 minutes or until just dry and cooked. Cool on the trays for 5 minutes, then transfer to wire racks to cool completely.

5 To make the caramel filling, whisk the dextrose in a saucepan over high heat until melted. Bring to the boil and cook for 2-3 minutes or until golden. Carefully whisk in the butter, then remove from the heat and whisk in the cream. Put the cornflour and water into a small jug and whisk until smooth, then add to the pan. Return the pan to low heat, then stir the mixture continuously for 3-4 minutes or until thickened. Leave to cool completely.

6 Spread the caramel filling over half of the cooled biscuits and sandwich with the remaining biscuits. Store in an airtight container for up to 2 days.

COCONUT MACAROONS

MAKES 18

3 egg whites
70g dextrose
250g shredded coconut
35g plain flour, sifted
1 teaspoon vanilla essence,
   or to taste

If you prefer the softer, white and chewy result that using untoasted coconut offers use this instead. Alternatively, you can toast the coconut before mixing it in with the egg and flour, if you favour a crisp and crunchy result.

1   Preheat the oven to 180°C (160°C fan-assisted). Line 2 baking trays with baking paper.

2   Whisk the egg whites with an electric mixer until soft peaks form. With the motor running, gradually add the dextrose, whisking until stiff peaks form. Fold in the coconut, flour and vanilla until well combined. Spoon tablespoons of the mixture onto the prepared trays.

3   Bake the macaroons for 15-20 minutes or until golden. Leave to cool on the trays. Store in an airtight container for up to 3 days.

PEANUT BISCUITS

MAKES 12

75g self-raising flour, sifted

75g plain flour, sifted

70g dextrose

125g peanuts, toasted and
 roughly chopped

1 egg, lightly beaten

100g unsalted butter, chopped
 and softened

1 teaspoon sea salt

These salty, nutty biscuits satisfy cravings for peanut cookies usually made with sugar-laden store-bought peanut butter.

1 Preheat the oven to 180°C (160°C fan-assisted). Line a baking tray with baking paper.

2 Put the self-raising flour, plain flour, dextrose and peanuts into a bowl. Add the egg and butter and mix until well combined.

3 Roll tablespoons of the mixture into balls, then put onto the prepared tray, leaving room between them for the mixture to spread. Press gently to flatten. Sprinkle with the salt.

4 Bake the biscuits for 15–20 minutes or until golden. Cool on the tray for 5 minutes, then transfer to a wire rack to cool completely. Store in an airtight container for up to 2 days.

COFFEE & CHOCOLATE BUTTERCREAM SANDWICHES

MAKES 16 SANDWICHES (32 BISCUITS)

185g unsalted butter, chopped and softened

135g dextrose, plus extra for dusting

1 teaspoon vanilla essence, or to taste

1 egg yolk, lightly beaten

1 tablespoon milk

60ml strong coffee

450g plain flour, sifted

Chocolate buttercream

150g unsalted butter, chopped

70g dextrose

2 tablespoons milk

2 tablespoons cocoa powder, sifted

2 teaspoons vanilla essence, or to taste

The coffee shortbreads can be eaten alone or sandwiched with the buttercream for a more indulgent treat.

1 Beat the butter, dextrose and vanilla with an electric mixer until light and creamy. Add the egg yolk, milk and coffee and beat until well combined. Add the flour and beat until just combined. Form the dough into a disc, then wrap in plastic film and refrigerate for 30 minutes.

2 Preheat the oven to 180°C (160°C fan-assisted). Line 2 baking trays with baking paper.

3 Roll out the dough between 2 sheets of baking paper until 5mm thick. Use a 5cm fluted cookie cutter to cut out rounds from the dough. Put onto the prepared baking trays, leaving room between for them to spread.

4 Bake the biscuits for 10-12 minutes or until just golden and cooked. Cool on the trays for 5 minutes, then transfer to wire racks to cool completely.

5 To make the buttercream, beat the butter, dextrose, milk, cocoa and vanilla with an electric mixer until light and creamy.

6 Spread the buttercream over half of the biscuits and sandwich with the remaining biscuits. Dust with extra dextrose, if you like. Store in an airtight container for up to 4 days.

CUPC
&C
&

AKES
AKES

VANILLA CUPCAKES

MAKES 12

120g unsalted butter, chopped
  and softened

135g dextrose

2 teaspoons vanilla essence,
  or to taste

2 eggs

300g self-raising flour, sifted

250ml milk

Italian meringue icing

50g unsalted butter, softened

105g dextrose

1 tablespoon water

2 egg whites

pinch of cream of tartar

» VARIATION :

  To make one large vanilla cake,
  lightly grease and line a 20cm
  cake tin with baking paper,
  then add the batter. Bake for
  35-40 minutes or until cooked
  when tested with a skewer.

The icing on these cupcakes has been caramelised with a kitchen blowtorch – you could replicate this effect by placing the iced cakes under a hot grill or leave as is. Alternatively, ice the cakes with the icing on page 192.

1   Preheat the oven to 180°C (160°C fan-assisted). Line a 12-hole muffin tin with paper cases.

2   Beat the butter, dextrose and vanilla with an electric mixer until light and creamy. With the motor running, add the eggs, beating until well combined. Alternately fold in the flour and milk until the batter is smooth. Spoon into the prepared cases.

3   Bake the cakes for 15-20 minutes or until cooked when tested with a skewer. Transfer to a wire rack to cool completely.

4   To make the icing, beat the butter with the electric mixer until light and creamy. Transfer to a clean bowl and set aside. Put the dextrose and water into a small saucepan and bring to the boil over medium heat, then cook until the syrup reaches soft ball stage (121°C on a confectionery thermometer). To test, place a drop of hot syrup in a cup of cold water – it should easily form a ball when rolled between 2 fingers. Whisk the egg whites and cream of tartar with the clean, dry electric mixer until soft peaks form. With the motor running, gradually pour in the dextrose syrup, continuing to whisk until the mixture is thick, glossy and cold. Add the butter and whisk until well combined.

5   Spread the icing on the cooled cupcakes and eat on the day they are made. Store uniced cakes in an airtight container in the freezer for up to 1 month.

MACADAMIA BROWNIES

SERVES 8-10

270g dextrose

4 eggs

250g unsalted butter, melted and cooled

185g plain flour, sifted

55g cocoa powder, sifted, plus extra for dusting

½ teaspoon baking powder, sifted

100g macadamias, toasted and roughly chopped

A brownie should still be soft in the centre so take care not to overcook; it will set as it cools. These brownies are on the cakey rather than fudgy side.

1 Preheat the oven to 180°C (160°C fan-assisted). Grease and line a 22cm square cake tin with baking paper.

2 Put the dextrose and eggs into a medium bowl and whisk until light and creamy. Add the melted butter, flour, cocoa and baking powder and stir to combine. Fold in the macadamias. Pour the batter into the prepared tin.

3 Bake for 35 minutes or until cooked but still soft in the centre. Leave to cool completely in the tin. Cut into squares, then dust with cocoa and serve. Store in an airtight container for up to 3 days.

- - - - - - - - - - - - - - - - - - - -

» VARIATION :

The addition of macadamias gives these brownies the extra crunch you would usually get from chocolate bits, but you can leave them out, or use other nuts such as almonds or walnuts, if you prefer.

SPONGE CAKE WITH JAM & CREAM

SERVES 8

225g unsalted butter, chopped and softened

135g dextrose, plus extra for dusting

1 teaspoon vanilla essence, or to taste

4 eggs

200g self-raising flour, sifted

25g cornflour, sifted

60ml milk

330g Roasted Strawberry & Rhubarb Jam (see page 190)

250ml double cream, whipped

》 VARIATION:

This sponge is equally delicious spread with the passionfruit or lemon curd on page 193 instead of jam.

We all need a fail-safe sponge recipe in our repertoire and this one fits the bill. While not quite as feather-light as the classic version, it is deliciously moist when filled with whipped cream and jam.

1   Preheat the oven to 180°C (160°C fan-assisted). Grease and line two 20cm springform cake tins with baking paper.

2   Beat the butter, dextrose and vanilla with an electric mixer until light and creamy. Add one egg at a time, beating well after adding each one. Fold in the flour and cornflour until well combined. Fold in the milk. Spoon the batter evenly into the prepared tins.

3   Bake the cakes for 20-25 minutes or until they come away from the edge of the tins. Leave the cakes to cool in the tins for 10 minutes, then turn out onto wire racks to cool completely.

4   Spread one cake with jam and cream, then top with the other cake and dust with extra dextrose. This cake is best eaten on the day it is made.

RED VELVET FAIRY CAKES

MAKES 12

200g unsalted butter, chopped and softened

270g dextrose, plus extra for dusting

1 teaspoon vanilla essence, or to taste

3 eggs

300g plain flour

25g cocoa powder

1 teaspoon bicarbonate of soda

250ml buttermilk

red food colouring, as needed

250ml double cream, whipped

- - - - - - - - - - - - - - - - - -

» VARIATION:

To make two large cakes, use 300g self-raising flour instead of the plain flour. Pour the batter into two greased and lined 20cm cake tins and bake for 35–40 minutes or until cooked when tested with a skewer.

You could ice the uncut tops of these tempting little cakes with the chocolate glaze on page 92 instead of filling them with whipped cream, if preferred.

1   Preheat the oven to 180°C (160°C fan-assisted). Line a 12 hole-capacity muffin tin with paper cases.

2   Beat the butter, dextrose and vanilla with an electric mixer until light and creamy. Add one egg at a time, beating well after adding each one.

3   Sift the flour, cocoa and bicarbonate of soda into a medium bowl and whisk until well combined. With the motor running, alternately add the flour mixture and buttermilk to the butter mixture and beat until just combined. Fold in the food colouring until the batter is your desired colour. Spoon evenly into the prepared paper cases.

4   Bake the cakes for 25–30 minutes or until cooked when tested with a skewer. Cool in the tin for 5 minutes, then transfer to a wire rack to cool completely.

5   Use a teaspoon to carefully scoop out the centre of each cupcake (see photo), reserving the tops. Spoon a tablespoon of whipped cream into each hole, then top with the reserved cake tops. (You can cut the reserved cake tops in half, then position them in the cream to resemble fairy wings, if you like.) Dust with extra dextrose. These cakes are best eaten on the day they are made. Store any leftover cakes wrapped in plastic film or freezer bags in an airtight container in the freezer for up to 1 month.

ALMOND TEA CAKE

SERVES 8-10

225g unsalted butter, chopped and softened

135g dextrose, plus extra for dusting

1 teaspoon vanilla essence, or to taste

2 tablespoons finely grated lemon zest

3 eggs

150g self-raising flour, sifted

1 teaspoon baking powder, sifted

200g ground almonds

125ml milk

whipped cream (optional), to serve

Serve this rich buttery cake with cream and raspberries for a special occasion or as is for afternoon tea – or just with cream...

1 Preheat the oven to 170°C (150°C fan-assisted). Lightly grease a 22cm round cake tin and line it with 2 layers of baking paper (this helps to prevent the edges from burning).

2 Beat the butter, dextrose, vanilla and lemon zest with an electric mixer until light and creamy. Add one egg at a time, beating well after adding each one. Add the flour, baking powder, ground almonds and milk and beat until well combined. Spoon the batter into the prepared tin.

3 Bake the cake for 30–35 minutes or until cooked when tested with a skewer. Leave to cool in the tin for 5 minutes, then turn out onto a wire rack to cool completely. Dust with extra dextrose to serve. Store in an airtight container in the fridge for up to 3 days.

ORANGE POLENTA CAKE

SERVES 8-10

185g unsalted butter, chopped and softened

135g dextrose

1 tablespoon finely grated orange zest

1 teaspoon vanilla essence, or to taste

3 eggs

225g self-raising flour, sifted

150g polenta

185ml milk

double cream (optional), to serve

Orange glaze

250ml water

135g dextrose

zest of 1 orange, removed with a vegetable peeler

The addition of polenta gives this orange-scented cake a wonderful, almost crunchy texture.

1   Preheat the oven to 180°C (160°C fan-assisted). Grease and line a 22cm ring cake tin with 2 layers of baking paper.

2   Beat the butter, dextrose, orange zest and vanilla with an electric mixer until light and creamy. Add one egg at a time, beating well after adding each one. Add the flour, polenta and milk and continue to beat until smooth and well combined. Spoon the batter into the prepared tin.

3   Bake the cake for 35-40 minutes or until cooked when tested with a skewer.

4   Meanwhile, to make the orange glaze, put the water, dextrose and orange zest into a small saucepan and bring to the boil over high heat. Simmer for 8-10 minutes or until thickened. Pour over the warm cake in the tin and leave to cool completely.

5   Serve the cake with double cream, if desired. Store in an airtight container for up to 2 days. Leftover slices of cake may be individually wrapped in plastic film or freezer bags and stored in an airtight container in the freezer for up to 1 month.

TARTS, TORT &

APPLE TARTE TATIN

SERVES 6-8

plain flour, for dusting
1 × 375g block butter puff pastry
135g dextrose
50g unsalted butter, chopped
4 pink lady apples, cored and
  cut into 8 wedges each
double cream or Custard
  (see page 192), to serve

You can use whatever size heavy-based ovenproof frying pan you have to make this classic French upside-down tart. Just be sure to cut the pastry round 2cm bigger than the diameter of your pan so there's enough pastry to tuck in the edges and cover the fruit.

1 Preheat the oven to 200°C (180°C fan-assisted).

2 Lightly dust a bench-top with flour, then roll out the pastry until 5mm thick. Use a dinner plate as a guide to cut out a pastry round, then set aside.

3 Heat the dextrose in a 22cm ovenproof non-stick frying pan over high heat, whisking until melted. Bring to the boil and continue to cook without stirring or touching until it turns a caramel colour. Carefully whisk in the butter. Immediately remove the pan from the heat and arrange the apple wedges on top.

4 Put the pastry over the apple, folding the edges under at the sides and tucking the apple in. Use a small sharp knife to make 3 small cuts in the centre of the pastry to allow steam to escape. Put the pan onto a baking tray to catch any overflowing juices.

5 Bake the tart for 25-30 minutes or until the pastry is puffed and golden. Leave to stand in the pan for 5 minutes, then turn out onto a plate. Serve with cream or custard.

» VARIATION:
  While it's traditional to use apples in tarte tatin, you could use another firm fruit such as pears or plums instead.

CHOCOLATE TORTE WITH COFFEE MASCARPONE

SERVES 6-8

110g unsalted butter, chopped and softened

270g dextrose

2 teaspoons vanilla essence, or to taste

4 eggs

300g self-raising flour, sifted

55g cocoa powder, sifted, plus extra for dusting

250ml milk

Coffee mascarpone

1 tablespoon instant coffee

1 tablespoon boiling water

250g mascarpone

70g dextrose

» VARIATION:

As this recipe makes 2 cakes you could halve the quantities to make a single chocolate cake (or make both cakes and freeze one for another time). Simply ice the cake with the chocolate icing on page 64 or the chocolate fudge icing on page 172.

If you are lucky enough to have any of this luscious cake left over, briefly heat slices in the microwave and serve them with the chocolate fudge sauce on page 191 and ice cream on page 124 for a wonderful dessert!

1 Preheat the oven to 180°C (160°C fan-assisted). Grease and line two 20cm round cake tins with 2 layers of baking paper.

2 Beat the butter, dextrose and vanilla with an electric mixer until light and creamy. Add one egg at a time, beating well after adding each one.

3 Add the flour, cocoa and milk and beat until the mixture is smooth and well combined. Spoon half of the batter into each of the prepared cake tins.

4 Bake the cakes for 50-60 minutes or until cooked when tested with a skewer. Turn out onto wire racks to cool completely.

5 Meanwhile, to make the coffee mascarpone, put the coffee and water into a small jug or bowl and stir until the coffee has dissolved. Put the mascarpone into a medium bowl and whisk until softened. Add the dextrose and the coffee mixture and mix until well combined.

6 Spread half of the mascarpone mixture onto one of the cooled cakes and top with the remaining cake and mascarpone. Dust with extra cocoa. This is best eaten on the day it is made. Store leftover slices of cake wrapped in plastic film or freezer bags in an airtight container in the freezer for up to 2 weeks.

RHUBARB COBBLERS

SERVES 6

500g rhubarb stalks, chopped
270g dextrose
2 star anise
1 cinnamon stick

Cobbler topping
150g self-raising flour, sifted
35g dextrose
1 teaspoon vanilla essence,
 or to taste
75g cold unsalted butter, chopped
60ml milk

Here is a quick alternative to a pastry-enclosed pie. If you're not keen on rhubarb then you can use the cobbler topping to cover any stewed fruit. Try serving this with the caramel sauce on page 67 or custard on page 192 – or both if you like!

1 Preheat the oven to 180°C (160°C fan-assisted).

2 Put the rhubarb, dextrose, star anise and cinnamon into a medium saucepan. Cook over medium heat, stirring for 5 minutes or until the dextrose has dissolved and the rhubarb has softened slightly. Remove and discard the cinnamon and star anise. Divide the rhubarb among six 375ml-capacity ramekins. Set aside.

3 To make the cobbler topping, mix the flour, dextrose and vanilla in a large bowl. Add the butter and, using your fingertips, rub it into the flour mixture until the mixture resembles fine breadcrumbs. Gradually add the milk, stirring until a dough forms. Divide the dough into 6 rounds to fit the tops of the ramekins. Place one on top of the rhubarb mixture in each ramekin.

4 Bake the cobblers for 30 minutes or until the topping is golden and cooked when tested with a skewer. Serve.

PASSIONFRUIT TARTLETS

MAKES 4

olive oil spray, for greasing
1 quantity Passionfruit Curd
  (see page 193)

Coconut pastry
150g plain flour
95g shredded coconut
35g dextrose
90g cold unsalted butter, chopped
1 egg yolk

The tropical touch of coconut in the pastry is a perfect match for the slight tang of the passionfruit curd filling. These tarts can be prepared in advance and refrigerated; just remove them from the fridge to return to room temperature for one to two hours before serving to make the passionfruit curd nice and soft.

1 To make the pastry, process the flour, coconut, dextrose, butter and egg yolk in a food processor until the mixture just comes together to form a dough. Gently press the dough into a disc, then wrap in plastic film and refrigerate for 30 minutes.

2 Preheat the oven to 180°C (160°C fan-assisted). Spray four 9cm tart tins with removable bases with olive oil spray.

3 Divide the dough into quarters, then roll out each piece until 5 mm thick and use to line the prepared tins. Prick the bases with a fork. Bake for 10-12 minutes or until crisp and golden. Leave to cool completely.

4 Spoon the passionfruit curd into the tartlet shells and serve.

» VARIATIONS:
For little lemon tarts, simply replace the passionfruit curd with the lemon curd on page 193. If you prefer to make one large tart, use a 21cm flan tin instead of individual tins and bake for 20-25 minutes or until golden.

PECAN PIE

SERVES 6

105g dextrose

125ml glucose syrup

40g unsalted butter

3 eggs

60ml double cream

2 teaspoons vanilla essence,
 or to taste

125g pecan halves

whipped cream,
 to serve (optional)

Sweet pastry

250g plain flour, sifted

2 tablespoons dextrose

¼ teaspoon baking powder, sifted

180g cold unsalted butter, chopped

60-100ml iced water

1½ teaspoons vanilla essence,
 or to taste

- - - - - - - - - - - - - - - - - - -

》 VARIATION:

You can also use the pastry
and filling to make individual
muffin-sized pecan pies using
a greased muffin tin. Bake for
25-30 minutes or until golden
and set.

Universally loved by sugar addicts and those who have
kicked the sugar habit, this is the perfect contribution
to the dessert table at your next celebration. If the filling
starts to become too dark, simply cover it with foil for the
remainder of the cooking time.

1 To make the pastry, process the flour, dextrose and baking
   powder in a food processor until combined. Add the butter and
   process until the mixture resembles fine breadcrumbs. With the
   motor running, gradually add the water and vanilla and process
   until the mixture comes together to form a smooth dough.
   Shape into a disc, then wrap in plastic film and refrigerate
   for 30 minutes.

2 Lightly grease a 34cm × 11cm rectangular tart tin. Roll the pastry
   out between 2 sheets of baking paper until 3mm thick. Line the
   prepared tin with the pastry. Trim the edges using a small, sharp
   knife. Refrigerate for 30 minutes.

3 Preheat the oven to 170°C (150°C fan-assisted).

4 Put the dextrose, glucose syrup and butter into a saucepan and
   stir over low heat for 2-3 minutes or until melted and combined.
   Transfer to a bowl, then add the eggs, cream and vanilla and
   whisk to combine. Pour into the tin and top with the pecans.
   Place the tin on a baking tray.

5 Bake the tart for 1 hour or until golden and set. Cool completely.
   Serve with cream, if desired. Store in an airtight container in the
   fridge for up to 2 days.

APPLE & RHUBARB PIE

SERVES 8-10

10 granny smith apples, cored
and roughly chopped

270g dextrose

2 teaspoons ground cinnamon

500g rhubarb stalks,
roughly chopped

1 quantity Sweet Pastry
(see page 80)

120g ground almonds

1 egg, beaten

Just the thing to cheer up your loved ones on a cold winter's night, this old-fashioned favourite is perfect served with the custard on page 192.

1 Put the apple, dextrose and cinnamon into a large saucepan. Cook over medium heat, stirring for 10-12 minutes. Add the rhubarb and cook for a further 5 minutes or until the fruit has softened but the apple still holds its shape. Leave to cool completely.

2 Preheat the oven to 200°C (180°C fan-assisted). Lightly grease a 20cm pie tin or dish.

3 Roll two-thirds of the pastry out between 2 sheets of baking paper until 3mm thick and use to line the pie dish. Roll the remaining pastry to make a 22cm round for the pie lid.

4 Scatter the ground almonds over the base of the pastry, then spoon over the apple and rhubarb filling. Top with the pie lid, trimming the edges with a small, sharp knife. Use a fork to seal the edges. Cut a small slit in the centre to allow steam to escape. Brush the lid with the beaten egg.

5 Bake the pie for 30-35 minutes or until the pastry is golden and cooked through. Serve warm.

» VARIATION:

If you are short of time, use 2 sheets of store-bought butter puff pastry instead of making your own.

CHILLED VANILLA CHEESECAKE

SERVES 6-8

500g cream cheese, chopped
2 tablespoons finely grated
  lemon zest
2 teaspoons vanilla essence,
  or to taste
200g dextrose
500ml double cream

Coconut base
115g plain flour, sifted
30g desiccated coconut
45g dextrose
100g unsalted butter, melted

This vanilla and lemon-scented cheesecake is everything a chilled cheesecake should be – soft, creamy and absolutely luscious. The set of this version is not as firm as a baked one, so it is best eaten straight from the fridge.

1   Preheat the oven to 170°C (150°C fan-assisted). Lightly grease a 22cm springform cake tin and line with baking paper.

2   To make the base, mix the flour, coconut, dextrose and butter in a bowl until combined. Press into the base of the prepared tin.

3   Bake the base for 20-25 minutes or until golden. Leave to cool completely.

4   Beat the cream cheese with an electric mixer for 4-5 minutes or until smooth. Add the lemon zest, vanilla and dextrose and beat until well combined.

5   Whisk the cream until soft peaks form, then gently fold through the cream cheese mixture until well combined. Spoon onto the cooked base in the tin and smooth the top. Refrigerate for 4-6 hours or until set. Store in an airtight container in the fridge for up to 2 days.

CHOCOLATE MOUSSE TART

SERVES 6-8

1 teaspoon powdered gelatine

60ml warm water

70g dextrose

30g cocoa powder, sifted,
  plus extra for dusting

250ml single cream

1 teaspoon vanilla essence,
  or to taste

whipped cream (optional),
  to serve

Chocolate pastry

75g plain flour, sifted

30g cocoa powder, sifted

30g desiccated coconut

45g dextrose

100g unsalted butter, melted

- - - - - - - - - - - - - - - - - -

» VARIATION:

If you like, replace the vanilla
essence with a few drops of
natural peppermint essence
for a choc-mint flavoured tart.

Although this tart is not overly sweet, for sugar-free converts the luscious texture and decadent chocolaty flavour of this mousse tart is guaranteed to tempt you.

1 Preheat the oven to 170°C (150°C fan-assisted). Grease a 20cm pie tin or deep tart tin with a removable base.

2 To make the chocolate pastry, process the flour, cocoa, coconut, dextrose and butter in a food processor until the mixture just comes together to form a dough. Press into the base and side of the prepared tart tin.

3 Bake the pastry for 20-25 minutes or until dry and dark brown. Leave to cool completely.

4 Meanwhile, place the gelatine in a small jug and pour over the warm water. Whisk with a fork until the gelatine has dissolved. Set aside for 1 minute.

5 Mix the dextrose and cocoa in a bowl. Add the cream and vanilla and whisk until soft peaks form. Add the gelatine mixture and whisk gently until well combined. Spoon into the cooled tart shell and refrigerate for 2-3 hours or until set. Top with whipped cream, if desired, then dust with extra cocoa and serve.

BAKLAVA

MAKES 18 PIECES

150g walnuts

150g peeled pistachios

35g dextrose

1 teaspoon ground cinnamon

180g unsalted butter, melted and cooled

1 × 375g packet filo pastry (it is impossible to buy filo that doesn't contain vegetable oil; however, you won't consume a significant quantity when you eat a few pieces of this)

2 teaspoons water

Clove syrup

25ml glucose syrup

100g dextrose

125ml water

finely grated zest of 1 lemon

6 cloves

- - - - - - - - - - - - - - - - - - -

» VARIATION:

If you don't have any whole cloves in your pantry use a cinnamon stick instead to make a cinnamon syrup.

The trick to making this is to buy refrigerated filo pastry.

1 To make the syrup, bring the glucose, dextrose, water, lemon zest and cloves to the boil in a saucepan over high heat, stirring until the dextrose has dissolved. Reduce the heat to medium and simmer for 3–5 minutes. Set aside to cool.

2 Preheat the oven to 180°C (160°C fan-assisted). Toast the walnuts on a baking tray for 5–8 minutes or until golden. Cool. Process the walnuts, pistachios, dextrose and cinnamon in a food processor until finely chopped.

3 Brush a 30cm × 20cm baking tin with butter. Unroll the filo on a chopping board and place the prepared tin on top. Use a small sharp knife to cut around the top of the tin all the way through the filo sheets. Discard the trimmings. Keep the filo covered with a clean, slightly damp tea towel to stop it from drying out.

4 Brush 1 filo sheet at a time with butter, then put into the tin. Repeat to create 9 layers of filo. Evenly scatter over one-third of the nut mixture. Repeat the buttering and layering process with another 6 filo sheets. Scatter over another third of the nuts and top with another 6 buttered and layered filo sheets. Scatter over the remaining nuts, then top with another 6 buttered filo sheets. Brush the top with melted butter. Freeze for 10 minutes, then use a small, sharp knife to score the top layers of filo in a diamond pattern and sprinkle the top with the water.

5 Bake the baklava for 30–35 minutes or until golden. Pour the syrup over the hot baklava and set aside to cool at room temperature for 2 hours. Cut to serve. This is best eaten on the day it is made.

DESS

ERTS

CHOCOLATE PROFITEROLES

MAKES 18

250ml water
80g unsalted butter, chopped
150g plain flour, sifted
3 eggs

Vanilla cream
250ml double cream
45g dextrose
1 teaspoon vanilla essence,
  or to taste

Chocolate glaze
30g cocoa powder, sifted
135g dextrose
2 tablespoons boiling water

These gorgeous little choux pastry treats are so delicious that even sugar addicts won't know they are sugar-free! Profiteroles are best eaten on the day they are made.

1   Preheat the oven to 200°C (180°C fan-assisted). Line 2 baking trays with baking paper.

2   Put the water and butter into a saucepan over high heat. Cook for 5 minutes or until the butter has melted and the mixture comes to the boil. Add the flour and beat with a wooden spoon until smooth. Cook the paste over low heat, stirring constantly for 2–3 minutes or until it comes away from the side of the pan. Remove the pan from the heat and add one egg at a time, beating with the wooden spoon after adding each one until the eggs are incorporated.

3   Spoon the choux pastry into a piping bag fitted with a 1cm nozzle. Pipe 4cm rounds onto the prepared trays. Bake for 20–25 minutes or until puffed and golden. Transfer to wire racks to cool completely.

4   To make the vanilla cream, whisk the cream, dextrose and vanilla in a bowl until soft peaks form. Make a small incision in each profiterole with a sharp knife, then spoon a tablespoon of the cream mixture into the centre.

5   To make the chocolate glaze, mix the cocoa, dextrose and water in a heatproof bowl, stirring until smooth. Dip the top of each profiterole into the glaze, then serve.

POACHED PEARS WITH BRIE

SERVES 4

270g dextrose
1.5 litres water
4 beurre bosc pears
1 vanilla bean, split and
    seeds scraped
ripe brie, to serve

Use this versatile syrup to poach your favourite seasonal fruit. The trick to poaching is to keep your liquid at a gentle simmer. Don't let it boil or your fruit will not cook evenly and keep its shape.

1   Put the dextrose and water into a saucepan. Stir over medium heat until the dextrose has dissolved. Simmer for 5 minutes or until the syrup has thickened slightly.

2   Peel the pears from the stem down, if you like. Add the pears and vanilla bean to the syrup. Cover with a piece of baking paper, then simmer over low heat for 15-20 minutes or until the pears are tender when tested with a skewer, turning occasionally to ensure even cooking.

3   Serve the pears warm or cooled with a little poaching liquid and soft brie alongside.

- -

» VARIATION:

Add whatever flavour you like to the syrup. If you're poaching plums, I suggest popping a drop of rosewater into the syrup. (Leave the skin of the fruit on for more fibre.)

CHOCOLATE FONDANTS

SERVES 6

250g unsalted butter, chopped

55g cocoa powder,
  plus extra for dusting

5 eggs

5 egg yolks

270g dextrose

250g plain flour, sifted

double cream, to serve (optional)

Making gooey chocolate fondants without using purchased chocolate has been a little tricky. However, through lots of experimenting we've discovered that the butter and cocoa in this mixture successfully recreate the soft, oozing chocolate 'volcano' experience you expect from a fondant.

1 Preheat the oven to 160°C (140°C fan-assisted). Grease and flour six 250ml-capacity ramekins.

2 Put the butter and cocoa into a heatproof bowl over a saucepan of boiling water and stir until melted and well combined, making sure the bottom of the bowl doesn't touch the water. Set aside to cool slightly.

3 Whisk the eggs, egg yolks and dextrose with an electric mixer until light and creamy. Pour the butter mixture into the egg mixture and stir to combine well. Gently fold in the flour until well combined. Spoon evenly into the prepared ramekins and set aside for 5-10 minutes.

4 Line the base of a large roasting tin with a tea towel folded to fit. Place the ramekins on the tea towel. Pour enough boiling water into the tin to reach halfway up the sides of the ramekins. Cover the roasting tin with foil.

5 Bake the fondants for 35-40 minutes or until the tops are cooked but the mixture is still soft in the centre. Remove the ramekins from the roasting tin and leave to set for 15 minutes. Dust generously with extra cocoa and serve with double cream, if desired.

PAVLOVA WITH BERRIES & PASSIONFRUIT

SERVES 6-8

olive oil spray, for greasing

4 egg whites

135g dextrose

3 teaspoons cornflour

1 teaspoon white vinegar

250ml double cream, whipped

125g strawberries, hulled and halved

125g raspberries

2-3 passionfruit, halved and pulp removed

» VARIATION:

Add a few drops of natural rosewater essence to the whipped cream for a rose-scented pavlova.

It is tricky to make pavlova without using sugar. After much experimenting, we've found it's really a matter of taking care not to overbeat the egg whites and allowing the meringue to dry out completely in the oven after turning the oven off. The extra cornflour also adds stability to the meringue. However, if your pavlova doesn't turn out picture-perfect, all is not lost – simply smash the meringue and serve it in glasses or cups with the cream and fruit for a delicious Eton mess.

1   Preheat the oven to 150°C (130° fan-assisted). Draw an 18cm round on a piece of baking paper, then put the paper upside-down onto a lightly sprayed baking tray.

2   Beat the egg whites with an electric mixer until soft peaks just form - do not overbeat. With the motor running, gradually add the dextrose, beating well until the meringue is glossy. Sift the cornflour over, then gently fold in the vinegar.

3   Mound the meringue onto the baking paper on the marked round. Put the baking tray into the oven, then immediately reduce the oven temperature to 120°C (100°C fan-assisted) and bake for 1 hour. Turn the oven off, then leave the meringue inside to cool completely.

4   Just before serving, transfer the meringue to a plate, then top with the whipped cream, berries and passionfruit pulp. Serve immediately. Pavlova is best eaten on the day it is made.

CREME CARAMEL

MAKES 4

200g dextrose
185ml milk
125ml double cream
2 eggs
1 egg yolk
2 tablespoons glucose syrup

The oozing caramel coating of this luscious custard always impresses when it appears on the dinner table.

1   Preheat the oven to 190°C (170°C fan-assisted).

2   Put 135g of the dextrose into a large frying pan. Stir over medium heat for 3-5 minutes until the dextrose has dissolved and turned golden. Pour evenly into four 125ml-capacity ramekins. Set aside.

3   Put the milk and cream into a medium saucepan. Bring just to the boil over medium heat. Remove from the heat.

4   Whisk the eggs, egg yolk, glucose and remaining dextrose in a large heatproof bowl until well combined. Gradually whisk in the milk mixture and carefully pour evenly into the ramekins.

5   Line the base of a large roasting tin with a tea towel folded to fit. Place the ramekins on the tea towel. Pour enough boiling water into the tin to reach halfway up the sides of the ramekins. Cover the roasting tin with foil.

6   Bake the custards for 40-45 minutes or until they are just set. Remove the ramekins from the tin and set aside for 2 hours to cool. Refrigerate for 2-3 hours.

7   To unmould, run a flat-bladed knife around the inside edge of each ramekin and carefully turn out each creme caramel onto a shallow bowl or serving plate. Serve.

» VARIATION:

To make a coconut version of creme caramel to top off an Asian-themed dinner party, replace the double cream with coconut cream and add some finely grated lime zest.

PASSIONFRUIT SOUFFLES

SERVES 6

melted butter, for greasing

100g dextrose, plus extra
for dusting

150ml passionfruit pulp (from
about 7 passionfruit)

1 tablespoon cornflour

3 teaspoons water

5 egg whites

Surprise your guests with these perfect passionfruit soufflés – they never fail to impress.

1   Preheat the oven to 180°C (160°C fan-assisted). Brush six 250ml-capacity ramekins generously with melted butter, then dust generously with extra dextrose and put onto a baking tray.

2   Put the passionfruit pulp and 35g of the dextrose into a small saucepan. Stir over low heat until the dextrose has dissolved. Increase the heat to high and bring to the boil.

3   Mix the cornflour and water in a small bowl to form a smooth paste. Remove the pan from the heat and whisk in the cornflour paste. Return the pan to the heat and cook, whisking continuously, for 1 minute. Transfer the mixture to a bowl and refrigerate until cold.

4   Whisk the egg whites with an electric mixer until foamy. Gradually add the remaining dextrose and continue to whisk just until stiff peaks form. Add a large spoonful of egg white to the passionfruit mixture and stir with a large metal spoon until combined to loosen the mixture. Gently fold in the remaining egg white.

5   Fill the ramekins to the top with the souffle mixture and run a palette knife across the top to make a flat surface. Run your thumb around the inside of the rim of each ramekin to help the souffles rise evenly.

6   Bake the souffles for 10-12 minutes or until risen and golden. Serve immediately.

BERRY CRUMBLE

SERVES 6-8

250g raspberries

250g blueberries

200g dextrose

1 tablespoon vanilla essence, or to taste

1 tablespoon finely grated lemon zest

double cream, to serve (optional)

Crumble topping

60g ground almonds

225g plain flour

135g dextrose

45g flaked almonds

180g unsalted butter, melted

Who doesn't love the appealing contrast of a soft fruit base and crisp topping that a crumble offers? Now you can be transported back to your childhood with this sugar-free topping.

1   Preheat the oven to 170°C (150°C fan-assisted).

2   Put the berries, dextrose, vanilla and lemon zest into a saucepan over medium heat and stir for 5 minutes or until the berries have softened but still hold their shape. Transfer to a 1 litre-capacity baking dish.

3   To make the crumble topping, mix the ground almonds, flour, dextrose, almonds and butter in a bowl, using your fingertips to rub in the butter until the mixture resembles very coarse crumbs. Scatter the crumble mixture evenly over the berries.

4   Bake the crumble for 30 minutes or until the topping is golden and cooked through. Serve with double cream, if desired.

》 VARIATION:

Crumble can be made with any fruit that is in season, such as apples, pears, plums or rhubarb.

CINNAMON & ORANGE SYLLABUB

SERVES 4

250ml dry white wine

135g dextrose

zest of 1 orange, removed in thick strips with a vegetable peeler

1 cinnamon stick

300ml double cream

orange segments (optional), to serve

Syllabub is a creamy English dessert traditionally made with wine, but you could flavour it with rum if you like. Just be careful not to overbeat your cream – soft peaks is all you need for this luscious dessert.

1 Put the wine, dextrose, orange zest and cinnamon into a medium saucepan. Bring to the boil over high heat, stirring until the dextrose has dissolved. Reduce the heat to medium and cook for 5-6 minutes. Remove from the heat and cool completely. Reserve ¼ of the syrup for drizzling. Remove and discard the orange zest and cinnamon.

2 Whisk the cream until soft peaks form. Fold in the remaining syrup and spoon into four 175ml glasses. Serve topped with orange segments and drizzled with reserved syrup, if you like.

BREAD & BUTTER PUDDING

SERVES 6

6 leftover Finger Buns (see page 151), sliced, or 22–24 thin slices brown bread

50g unsalted butter, softened

6 eggs, lightly beaten

250ml milk

125ml double cream

75g dextrose

cocoa powder, for dusting (optional)

Comfort food to warm the soul – and a terrific way to use up leftover finger buns, or brown bread from your favourite bakery. All recipes using custard should be cooked in a water bath to ensure a nice creamy and smooth texture.

1 Preheat the oven to 160°C (140°C fan-assisted).

2 Put the sliced finger buns onto a clean surface and spread evenly with the butter. Arrange, buttered-side up, in a 1.5 litre-capacity baking dish in overlapping rows.

3 Whisk the eggs, milk, cream and dextrose in a large bowl. Strain through a fine sieve into a jug. Pour evenly over the finger bun slices. Set aside for 15 minutes to soak.

4 Put the baking dish into a large roasting tin. Pour enough boiling water into the tin to come halfway up the side of the baking dish.

5 Bake the pudding for 35–40 minutes or until the custard has just set. Dust with cocoa, if desired, then serve warm.

- - - - - - - - - - - - - - - - - - -

>> VARIATION:

If you happen to have made the sugar-free chocolate on page 168, then roughly chop some and add it to the mixture before baking.

STICKY TOFFEE PUDDINGS

MAKES 4

75g unsalted butter, melted
70g dextrose
2 eggs, lightly beaten
120g ground almonds
150g plain flour, sifted
1 teaspoon baking powder
100ml milk
1 teaspoon vanilla essence,
  or to taste

Toffee syrup
200g dextrose
50g unsalted butter, chopped
2 tablespoons double cream

If you are a fan of toffee, you will really enjoy these indulgent little puddings, perfect for a quick mid-week pick-me-up after dinner.

1 Preheat the oven to 180°C (160°C fan-assisted). Grease four 175ml-capacity ovenproof moulds or ramekins.

2 Mix the butter, dextrose, egg, ground almonds, flour, baking powder, milk and vanilla in a large bowl until smooth and well combined.

3 Spoon the batter evenly into the prepared moulds or ramekins, then put onto a baking tray to catch any overflowing syrup.

4 Bake the puddings for 30–35 minutes or until the tops are golden and the puddings are cooked through when tested with a skewer.

5 Meanwhile, to make the toffee syrup, put the dextrose into a large frying pan and cook over medium heat for 2 minutes or until melted and golden. Carefully whisk in the butter and the cream until well combined and smooth, then pour over the puddings immediately. Serve hot.

FIVE-MINUTE CHOCOLATE CUP PUDDINGS

MAKES 4

125ml milk

100ml olive oil

1 tablespoon vanilla essence, or to taste

2 eggs

90g dextrose

75g self-raising flour, sifted

25g cocoa powder, sifted, plus extra for dusting

whipped cream, to serve

I really love this pudding. It's just the thing for when you're looking for a quick chocolate hit but don't have the time or inclination to make anything too complicated. Just be careful not to overcook it or you'll lose the luscious texture.

1   Whisk the milk, oil, vanilla and eggs in a bowl until smooth. Add the dextrose, flour and cocoa and whisk until well combined and smooth.

2   Pour into four 175ml microwave-safe mugs or tea cups. Cook in the microwave on medium power for 1 minute or until just cooked. Dust with extra cocoa, then top with a spoonful of cream and serve.

- - - - - - - - - - - - - - - - - - - -

» VARIATION:

For jaffa-flavoured puddings, stir some finely grated orange zest into the batter before cooking.

CHERRY TRIFLE

SERVES 6-8

110g unsalted butter, chopped
and softened

70g dextrose, plus extra
for dusting

1 teaspoon vanilla essence,
or to taste

2 eggs

100g self-raising flour, sifted

2 tablespoons cornflour, sifted

2 tablespoons milk

250ml double cream, whipped

1 quantity Poached Cherries
(see page 192)

cherries (optional), to serve

Vanilla custard

500ml double cream

250ml milk

1 teaspoon vanilla essence,
or to taste

6 egg yolks

200g dextrose

» VARIATION:
Try flavouring the custard with
ground spices such as cinnamon
or cloves or stir in some cocoa
powder for a chocolate custard.

1   Preheat the oven to 180°C (160°C fan-assisted). Grease and line
two 18cm springform cake tins with baking paper.

2   Beat the butter, dextrose and vanilla with an electric mixer until
light and creamy. Add one egg at a time, beating well after adding
each one. Fold in the flour and cornflour until well combined. Fold
in the milk. Spoon the batter into the prepared tins.

3   Bake the cakes for 20-25 minutes or until they pull away from
the edges of the tins. Leave to cool in the tins for 10 minutes,
then turn out onto wire racks to cool completely.

4   To make the custard, put the cream, milk and vanilla into
a heavy-based saucepan. Bring just to the boil over medium
heat. Whisk the egg yolks and dextrose in a large heatproof
bowl until the dextrose has dissolved. Gradually whisk the cream
mixture into the egg yolk mixture until well combined. Transfer
the custard to a clean heavy-based saucepan and cook over
medium heat, stirring continuously, for 8-10 minutes or until the
mixture is thick enough to coat the back of a spoon. Strain into
a bowl, cover closely with plastic film and refrigerate until cold.

5   To assemble, cut the sponges in half widthways. Put one layer
of sponge into a 1.5 litre-capacity glass dish (mine is 20cm
round). Top with some of the custard, another layer of sponge
and some of the cream, then top with the poached cherries and
their syrup. Top the cherries with another layer of sponge and
custard, then finish with the final layer of cake and cream.

6   Set aside for 2 hours to allow the flavours to soak into the
sponge (refrigerate if it's a hot day). Serve, topped with fresh
cherries, if you like.

EASTER TREATS

ICE CR
SOR
& JELL

EAMS

BET.

.IES

ICE CREAM SUNDAES WITH PISTACHIO TOFFEE

MAKES 1 LITRE

500ml double cream

250ml milk

1 teaspoon vanilla essence, or to taste

65ml glucose syrup

6 egg yolks

135g dextrose

1 quantity Hot Chocolate Fudge Sauce (see page 191)

Pistachio toffee

135g dextrose

65g pistachios, chopped

Use this vanilla-scented custard base to make any flavoured ice cream you like. The pistachio toffee adds a crunchy texture, but you can simply top the sundaes with pistachios.

1 Put the cream, milk and vanilla into a heavy-based saucepan and bring just to the boil over medium heat. Stir through the glucose until dissolved and well combined.

2 Whisk the egg yolks and dextrose in a large bowl until the dextrose has dissolved. Gradually whisk in the cream mixture until well combined.

3 Transfer the custard mixture to a clean saucepan and cook over medium heat, stirring continuously, for 8–10 minutes or until the mixture is thick enough to coat the back of a spoon. Strain into a bowl, cover closely with plastic film and refrigerate until cold.

4 Transfer the custard mixture to an ice-cream machine and churn according to the manufacturer's directions until frozen. Spoon into a 1 litre-capacity loaf tin and freeze for 2–3 hours or until hard. (Alternatively, you can scoop it directly from the ice-cream machine if you like soft-serve ice cream.)

5 To make the pistachio toffee, put the dextrose into a large non-stick frying pan and cook over medium heat for 4–5 minutes or until melted and golden. Pour onto a baking tray lined with baking paper, sprinkle over the pistachios and leave to cool for 10 minutes or until crisp. Break into large pieces.

6 Scoop the ice cream into sundae glasses or serving bowls, then top with the hot fudge sauce and pistachio toffee. Serve.

RHUBARB CRUMBLE ICE CREAM

MAKES 1 LITRE

250g rhubarb stalks,
   cut into 5cm lengths

270g dextrose

250ml double cream

250ml sour cream

250ml milk

1 teaspoon vanilla essence,
   or to taste

6 egg yolks

Almond crumble

30g ground almonds

115g plain flour

70g dextrose

90g unsalted butter, melted

- - - - - - - - - - - - - - - - - -

» VARIATION:

In addition to, or instead of, rhubarb, you could stir through raspberries, blueberries or any slightly softened fruit you like.

Your guests will love the contrasting textures of this sweet-and-sour ice cream with a crunchy crumble topping.

1 Preheat the oven to 160°C (140°C fan-assisted). Line a baking tray with baking paper.

2 To make the almond crumble, mix the almonds, flour, dextrose and butter in a medium bowl until the mixture resembles very coarse breadcrumbs. Spread out on the prepared tray and bake for 15-20 minutes or until golden. Set aside to cool.

3 Put the rhubarb and ½ of the dextrose into a medium saucepan. Cook over medium heat for 5-8 minutes or until the rhubarb has softened. Transfer to a bowl and leave to cool.

4 Put the cream, sour cream, milk and vanilla into a heavy-based saucepan. Bring just to the boil over medium heat. Whisk the egg yolks and remaining dextrose in a large bowl until the dextrose has dissolved. Gradually whisk in the cream mixture until well combined. Transfer to a clean saucepan and cook over medium heat, stirring continuously for 8-10 minutes or until the mixture is thick enough to coat the back of a spoon. Strain into a bowl, cover closely with plastic film and refrigerate until cold.

5 Transfer the custard to an ice-cream machine and churn according to manufacturer's directions until frozen. Add the rhubarb to the ice-cream machine and continue to churn for 5 minutes or until well combined. Transfer to a 1 litre-capacity loaf tin lined with plastic film and smooth the top. Top with the crumble, then wrap with plastic film and freeze for 2 hours or until set. Store in the freezer for up to 1 week.

VANILLA YOGHURT & PASSIONFRUIT JELLIES

MAKES 8

500g natural live yoghurt

35g dextrose

2 teaspoons vanilla essence, or to taste

2 tablespoons water

2 teaspoons powdered gelatine

Passionfruit jelly

12 passionfruit, halved and pulp removed

60ml water

2 tablespoons dextrose

2 teaspoons powdered gelatine

Make this pretty dessert ahead of time for a dinner party or simply to have in the fridge for cooling mid-week snacks and desserts.

1 Whisk together the yoghurt, dextrose and vanilla in a medium bowl. Put the water into a small jug and sprinkle over the gelatine. Set aside for 5 minutes to dissolve. Whisk the gelatine mixture into the yoghurt mixture. Spoon evenly into eight 175ml serving glasses. Refrigerate for 2 hours or until set.

2 To make the passionfruit jelly, put the passionfruit pulp, water and dextrose into a saucepan. Bring just to the boil. Remove from the heat and stir in the gelatine until dissolved. Spoon evenly over the set yoghurt jellies, then refrigerate for 2 hours or until set. Serve.

COCONUT & LIME SORBET

SERVES 4

200g dextrose

500ml water

1 lime, zest removed in wide strips with a vegetable peeler

500ml coconut milk

Living in Queensland it gets very steamy during summer. It's great to have a refreshing iced treat like this in the freezer to cool down on those balmy summer days – and nights.

1   Put the dextrose, water and lime zest into a medium saucepan. Stir over low heat until the dextrose has dissolved. Increase the heat to medium and simmer for 5 minutes. Stir in the coconut milk. Remove from the heat and cool completely.

2   Pour into an ice-cream machine and churn according to manufacturer's directions until frozen. Spoon into 4 glasses to serve. Store in an airtight container in the freezer for up to 2 weeks.

- - - - - - - - - - - - - - - - - - - -

》 VARIATION:

If you do not have an ice cream machine, use hand-held electric beaters to beat the sorbet every 2 hours, returning the mixture to the freezer each time, until the mixture is frozen.

MELON ICE LOLLIES

MAKES 8

These icy poles can be made with any pureed whole fruit you or your kids like.

70g dextrose
125ml water
1 lime, zest removed in wide strips
1 large cantaloupe, peeled,
    seeded and chopped

1   Put the dextrose, water and lime zest into a small saucepan. Stir the mixture over high heat until the dextrose has dissolved. Transfer to a bowl and refrigerate for 1 hour or until cold. Strain and discard the lime zest.

2   Blend the cantaloupe in a food processor until a smooth puree forms. Add the dextrose syrup and blend until well combined.

3   Divide the mixture among 8 ice lolly moulds. Put into the freezer overnight or until frozen. Store in the freezer for up to 1 month.

>> VARIATION:

If you don't have ice lolly moulds, simply put the mixture into glasses, sprayed with olive oil spray, or disposable cups and place a lolly stick in the middle.

MILKY-WAY ICE LOLLIES

MAKES 6

Kids both big and small will love these creamy treats.

625ml milk
1 tablespoon cornflour
1 teaspoon vanilla essence, or to taste
70g dextrose
125ml double cream

1   Whisk 60ml of the milk and the cornflour in a small bowl until the cornflour has dissolved.

2   Put the vanilla and remaining milk into a small saucepan. Bring just to the boil over medium heat. Add the cornflour mixture and dextrose and cook, stirring for 4-5 minutes. Add the cream and stir until well combined.

3   Transfer the mixture to a heatproof bowl, then cover with plastic film and refrigerate until cold.

4   Divide among 6 ice lolly moulds. Put into the freezer overnight or until frozen. Store in the freezer for up to 1 month.

CHOCOLATE ICE CREAM CONES

MAKES 10

500ml double cream

250ml milk

1 teaspoon vanilla essence, or to taste

60ml glucose syrup

6 egg yolks

135g dextrose

25g cocoa powder, sifted

Chocolate cones

100g unsalted butter, chopped and softened

135g dextrose

4 egg whites, lightly beaten

75g plain flour, sifted

25g cocoa powder, sifted

» VARIATION:

Push the hot waffles into muffin tin holes to make tuille baskets for your ice cream.

If you're short of time, you could just make the ice cream and serve it in bowls – I'm sure you won't get any complaints!

1 Put the cream, milk and vanilla into a heavy-based saucepan. Bring just to the boil over medium heat. Stir in the glucose until melted and well combined.

2 Whisk the egg yolks, dextrose and cocoa in a large bowl until the dextrose has dissolved. Gradually whisk in the cream mixture until well combined. Transfer to a clean saucepan and cook over medium heat, stirring continuously, for 8-10 minutes or until the mixture is thick enough to coat the back of a spoon. Strain into a bowl, cover closely with plastic film and refrigerate until cold.

3 Pour into an ice-cream machine, churn and freeze according to the manufacturer's instructions.

4 To make the cones, preheat the oven to 180°C (160°C fan-assisted). Grease and line a baking tray with baking paper.

5 Beat the butter and dextrose with an electric mixer until light and creamy. With the motor running, gradually add the egg whites, flour and cocoa and continue to beat until a batter forms. Spoon 2 teaspoons of the batter at a time onto the prepared tray and spread very thinly with a palette knife to form a round shape. Bake for 6-8 minutes or until cooked and dry. Working very quickly, curl each one around with your hands to form a cone. Set aside to cool. (Makes 10. If the waffle cones soften, freeze for an hour or so to crisp again.)

6 Scoop the ice cream into the cones and serve.

CHEAT'S VANILLA ICE CREAM & CHOCOLATE CHIP SANDWICHES

MAKES 8

500ml milk

500ml double cream

170g dextrose

4 egg yolks

2 teaspoons vanilla essence, or to taste

190g chopped Sugar-free Chocolate (see page 168)

16 wafers (available from the biscuit section of supermarkets)

cocoa powder, for dusting

I love how easy it is to make your own ice cream without having to start off by making a custard. However, this recipe uses raw eggs. If you're not comfortable with this, you can use the milk, cream, dextrose, egg yolks and vanilla to make a cooked custard base, following the instructions on page 134. These chocolate-studded ice cream sandwiches are a terrific way to use packaged wafers, which are almost sugar-free (0.02 grams per wafer). Unfortunately, the wafers aren't free from seed oils, but you won't consume a significant quantity if you have a couple of these delicious sandwiches.

1 Whisk the milk, cream, dextrose, egg yolks and vanilla in a large bowl until smooth. Pour into an ice-cream machine, churn and freeze according to the manufacturer's directions. Stir in the chopped chocolate until well combined.

2 Put 8 wafers into a 30cm × 20cm slice tin, then cover with a thick layer of ice cream. Top with the remaining 8 wafers and put into the freezer for 2–3 hours or until frozen.

3 Use a knife to evenly trim the sandwiches and carefully separate them. Serve dusted with cocoa. Store any leftover sandwiches in an airtight container in the freezer for up to 1 month.

KIDS' LUNCH &

BOX
PARTY
FARE

BLUEBERRY & CINNAMON OAT SQUARES

MAKES 24 SQUARES

180g quick-cook oats
75g self-raising flour
50g desiccated coconut
125g blueberries
2 teaspoons ground cinnamon
80g unsalted butter, chopped
180ml rice malt syrup
70g dextrose

This is one of my kids' favourites! Just make sure you allow the slice to cool at room temperature before cutting.

1   Preheat the oven to 180°C (160°C fan-assisted). Grease and line a 30cm × 20cm slice tin with baking paper.

2   Mix the oats, flour, coconut, blueberries and cinnamon in a large bowl.

3   Put the butter, syrup and dextrose into a saucepan. Stir frequently over low heat for 6-8 minutes or until the butter has melted and mixture is well combined. Pour over the oat mixture. Stir until well combined. Spoon the mixture into the prepared tin, using damp hands or the back of a spoon to smooth the surface.

4   Bake the slice for 25-30 minutes or until golden. Cool completely in the tin. Cut into squares to serve. Store in an airtight container in the fridge for up to 2 days.

CHOCOLATE CRACKLES

MAKES 12

250g cocoa butter
80g puffed rice
100g dextrose
2 tablespoons cocoa
  powder, sifted
70g desiccated coconut

Quick and easy to make, this nostalgic treat is an all-time favourite for kids' birthday parties and cake stalls. Puffed rice is available from supermarkets and health food stores.

You'll also find cocoa butter in most health food stores; however, be warned, it can be quite expensive.

1 Line twelve 125ml muffin tin holes with paper cases.

2 Melt the cocoa butter in a saucepan over low heat. Mix the puffed rice, dextrose, cocoa and coconut in a bowl. Pour in the melted cocoa butter and stir until well combined.

3 Spoon the mixture evenly into the prepared paper cases. Refrigerate for 2 hours or until set. Store in an airtight container in the fridge for up to 4 days.

MARSHMALLOWS

MAKES ABOUT 30

270g dextrose

350ml water

2 tablespoons gelatine

1 teaspoon vanilla essence,
  or to taste

red food colouring, as needed
  (optional)

35g cornflour

These fluffy marshmallows are a cinch to make with the kids. Serve them instead of lollies at a kid's party and watch them disappear.

1 Grease and line two 30cm × 20cm slice tins with baking paper.

2 Put 200g of the dextrose and 150ml of the water into a medium saucepan. Cook over medium heat, stirring frequently, for 3-5 minutes or until the dextrose has dissolved.

3 Put the gelatine and remaining 200ml water into a jug and stir until the gelatine has dissolved. Carefully pour into the pan of hot dextrose syrup. Stir over medium heat for 2-3 minutes or until the gelatine has dissolved.

4 Beat the gelatine mixture and vanilla with an electric mixer for 8-10 minutes or until thick. Spoon half of the mixture into one of the prepared tins and smooth the top. Add a little red food colouring to the remaining mixture, if desired, then spoon into the second tin and smooth the top. Set aside at room temperature for 1 hour or until set.

5 Mix the cornflour and remaining dextrose in a small bowl until well combined.

6 Remove the marshmallow from the tins and use a 6cm cookie cutter to cut it into 30 rounds. Put each marshmallow into the dextrose and cornflour mixture and roll gently to coat. Serve. Store in an airtight container in a cool, dry place for up to 2 days.

CINNAMON DOUGHNUTS

MAKES 10

2 teaspoons dried yeast

1½ tablespoons warm water

125ml warm milk

2 tablespoons dextrose, plus ¼ cup extra for dusting

50g unsalted butter, melted

335g plain flour, sifted, plus extra for dusting

1 teaspoon ground nutmeg

2 eggs, lightly beaten

2 tablespoons ground cinnamon

800g lard or solidified cooking oil (blended animal fat), for deep-frying

- - - - - - - - - - - - - - - - - -

» VARIATION:
To make iced doughnuts simply omit the cinnamon coating and ice with the chocolate glaze on page 92 instead.

Hot doughnuts fresh out of the pan are one of life's special treats and these cinnamon coated ones won't disappoint.

1 Put the yeast, water, milk and 3 level teaspoons of the dextrose in a large bowl and set aside in a warm place for 10 minutes or until bubbles appear on the surface.

2 Add the butter, flour, nutmeg, egg and remaining dextrose to the yeast mixture and use a butter knife to mix until a sticky dough forms.

3 Turn out the dough onto a lightly floured surface and knead until smooth. Put the dough into a lightly oiled bowl, cover with a clean, damp tea towel and set aside in a warm place for 45 minutes or until doubled in size. Meanwhile, mix the cinnamon and extra dextrose in a small bowl until well combined. Set aside.

4 Knead the dough on a lightly floured surface for 5 minutes or until smooth and elastic. Roll the dough into a log, then divide into 10 even portions and shape into rounds. Place the rounds on a baking tray lined with baking paper, cover with the tea towel and set aside for 30 minutes or until risen. Use the handle of a wooden spoon to poke a hole in the centre of each round.

5 Place the lard and a confectionery thermometer in a large deep saucepan over medium heat until the lard melts and registers 180°C on the thermometer. Cook the doughnuts, in batches, for 1-2 minutes on each side or until golden. Drain briefly on paper towel.

6 Dust the hot doughnuts with the cinnamon mixture and serve immediately.

BANANA BREAD

SERVES 8-10

135g dextrose

2 eggs

125ml olive oil

2 teaspoons vanilla essence,
or to taste

185g plain flour, sifted

1 teaspoon bicarbonate of
soda, sifted

2 teaspoons ground cinnamon

2 bananas, mashed

80g pecans (optional), toasted and
roughly chopped

butter (optional), to serve

If you're making this for the kids' lunch-boxes or any occasion where nut allergies may be an issue, simply omit the pecans.

1 Preheat the oven to 170°C (150°C fan-assisted). Grease and line a 21cm × 9cm loaf tin with baking paper.

2 Beat the dextrose, eggs, oil and vanilla with an electric mixer until light and creamy. Fold in the flour, bicarbonate of soda and cinnamon until just combined. Fold in the banana and pecans, if using. Spoon the batter into the prepared tin.

3 Bake the bread for 35-40 minutes or until cooked when tested with a skewer. Cool in the tin for 5 minutes, then turn out onto a wire rack to cool completely. Serve with butter, if desired. Store leftover slices individually wrapped in plastic film or freezer bags in an airtight container in the freezer for up to 1 month.

» VARIATION:
You can use walnuts or hazelnuts instead of pecans, if you prefer.

CHOCOLATE COCONUT SLICE

MAKES 16

150g self-raising flour, sifted

135g dextrose

50g desiccated coconut, plus extra for sprinkling

1 tablespoon cocoa powder, sifted

125g unsalted butter, melted

1 egg, lightly beaten

1 teaspoon vanilla essence, or to taste

Cocoa icing

135g dextrose

1 tablespoon cocoa powder

20g unsalted butter, softened

1 tablespoon milk

- - - - - - - - - - - - - - - - - -

》 VARIATIONS:

Try adding some pecans or almonds for extra crunch if you don't have any nut allergies to worry about. Use gluten-free self-raising flour if your children are gluten-intolerant.

Enjoy this sugar-free chocolate and coconut slab cake in slice form!

1 Preheat the oven to 180°C (160°C fan-assisted). Grease and line a 30cm × 20cm slice tin.

2 Mix the flour, dextrose, coconut and cocoa in a large bowl until well combined. Make a well in the centre, then add the butter, egg and vanilla and mix until well combined. Spoon into the prepared tin, then smooth the top.

3 Bake the cake for 20 minutes or until set. Leave in the tin to cool a little, then refrigerate for 2 hours or until completely cold.

4 Meanwhile, to make the icing, beat the dextrose, cocoa, butter and milk with an electric mixer until smooth and thick.

5 Spread the icing over the cold slice, then sprinkle with extra coconut. Cut into sixteen 9cm × 3cm bars. Serve. Store in an airtight container for up to 3 days.

BIRTHDAY TREATS

HOLI
TREA

AUSTRALIA DAY LAMINGTONS

MAKES 24

225g unsalted butter, chopped and softened

135g dextrose, plus extra for dusting

1 teaspoon vanilla essence, or to taste

4 eggs

200g self-raising flour, sifted

35g cornflour, sifted

60ml milk

250-350g desiccated coconut, as needed

Chocolate icing

270g dextrose

85g cocoa powder

185g boiling water

50g unsalted butter, melted

What could be more perfect to take to an Australia Day barbecue or picnic than these iconic little lamingtons? And no one will guess they don't contain sugar!

1 Preheat the oven to 180°C (160°C fan-assisted). Grease and line a 30cm × 20cm slice tin with baking paper.

2 Beat the butter, dextrose and vanilla with an electric mixer until light and creamy. Add one egg at a time, beating well after adding each one; the mixture will look like it has split but it will be okay. Fold in the flour and cornflour until well combined. Fold in the milk. Spoon the batter into the prepared tin.

3 Bake the cake for 20-25 minutes or until cooked when tested with a skewer. Leave to cool in the tin for 10 minutes, then turn out onto a wire rack to cool completely.

4 To make the icing, put the dextrose, cocoa, boiling water and butter into a heatproof bowl, then whisk until smooth.

5 Trim the top and edges of the sponge with a large serrated knife, then cut into 4 widthways and 6 lengthways to yield 24 pieces. Gently roll each piece in extra dextrose, then in the icing to coat. Gently roll in the coconut to evenly coat all sides; use half of the coconut at a time to prevent it from becoming stained with the icing. Leave on a wire rack for the coating to set.

6 Serve on the day they are made or wrap individually in plastic film or freezer bags and store in an airtight container in the freezer for up to 2 weeks.

HOT CROSS BUNS

MAKES 12

600g plain flour, plus extra
   for dusting
1 tablespoon mixed spice
2 × 7g sachets dried yeast
35g dextrose
pinch of salt
40g unsalted butter
300ml milk
2 eggs, lightly beaten
olive oil spray, for greasing

Flour paste
75g plain flour
90ml water

Glaze
125ml water
2 tablespoons dextrose

- - - - - - - - - - - - - - - - - - - -

》 VARIATION:

If you like, knead some finely
grated orange zest into the
dough before baking.

If you love hot cross buns, now you don't have to miss out.

1   Sift the flour and mixed spice into a large bowl, then add the
    yeast, dextrose and salt. Melt the butter in a small saucepan.
    Add the milk, then heat for 1 minute or until lukewarm. Add
    the warm milk mixture and egg to the flour mixture. Use a flat-
    bladed knife to mix until the dough almost comes together. Use
    clean hands to form a soft dough.

2   Knead the dough on a lightly floured surface for 5–10 minutes
    or until smooth. Transfer to a lightly oiled bowl. Cover with
    a clean tea towel. Set aside in a warm place for 1 hour or until
    doubled in size. Line a large baking tray with baking paper.

3   Punch the dough down to its original size. Knead on a lightly floured
    surface until smooth. Divide into 12 balls and put onto the prepared
    tray about 1cm apart. Cover loosely with plastic film. Set aside in
    a warm place for 30 minutes or until doubled in size.

4   Preheat the oven to 200°C (180°C fan-assisted).

5   For the paste, mix the flour and water until smooth, adding
    a little more water if needed. Spoon into a small snap-lock bag
    and snip off 1 corner. Pipe flour paste crosses on top of the buns.

6   Bake the hot cross buns for 15 minutes or until they are golden
    and cooked through.

7   For the glaze, stir the water and dextrose in a small saucepan
    over low heat until the dextrose has dissolved. Boil for 5 minutes.
    Brush the warm glaze over the warm hot cross buns. Serve.

CHOCOLATE EASTER NESTS

MAKES 16

250g cocoa butter

8 shredded wheat 'biscuits', roughly chopped

135g dextrose

2 tablespoons cocoa powder, sifted

Let the kids help mix and shape these fun Easter nests. They can be as creative as they like when the time comes to decorate them. You can wrap them in cellophane as your sugar-free contribution to an Easter egg hunt.

1 Line 2 baking trays with baking paper.

2 Melt the cocoa butter in a medium saucepan over low heat.

3 Put the shredded wheat, dextrose and cocoa into a medium bowl and mix until combined. Pour in the melted cocoa butter and stir until well combined.

4 Put tablespoons of the mixture onto the prepared trays. Use a teaspoon to push down in the centre to create the shape of a nest. Leave to cool and set at room temperature for 1 hour.

5 Decorate with small novelty chicks or other Easter-themed items, if desired. Store in an airtight container for up to 2 days.

SUGAR-FREE CHOCOLATE

MAKES 36 CHOCOLATES

80g cocoa butter (available from health food stores), chopped

80g cocoa powder, sifted

Dextrose syrup

135g dextrose

250ml water

Making your own chocolate at home is easier than you might think, especially if you have your own chocolate moulds. I encourage you to give this a go – you will never miss bought chocolate again.

1 To make the dextrose syrup, put the dextrose and water into a small saucepan and stir over medium heat until the dextrose has dissolved and the mixture is well combined. (Makes about 1 cup. Store any leftover syrup in an airtight container in the fridge for up to 1 month.)

2 Put the cocoa butter into a heatproof bowl over a saucepan of boiling water and stir until melted. Add the cocoa and 60ml of the dextrose syrup and stir until melted and well combined.

3 Pour the chocolate mixture into tablespoon-sized chocolate moulds. Refrigerate for 2-3 hours or until set. Store in an airtight container in the fridge for up to 2 weeks.

》 VARIATION:

You can use glucose syrup instead of homemade dextrose syrup, if you prefer.

GREEK EASTER BISCUITS

MAKES ABOUT 16

250g unsalted butter, chopped and softened

70g dextrose, plus extra for dusting

2 teaspoons ground allspice

1 teaspoon vanilla essence, or to taste

375g plain flour, sifted

60g ground almonds

This traditional Greek Easter treat is a great sweet alternative for when everyone has had enough chocolate!

1 Beat the butter, dextrose, allspice and vanilla with an electric mixer and until light and creamy. Fold in the flour and ground almonds until well combined. Wrap in plastic film and refrigerate for 30 minutes.

2 Preheat the oven to 160°C (140°C fan-assisted). Line 2 baking trays with baking paper.

3 Working with 2 tablespoonfuls of the dough at a time, roll into a short log, then bend slightly to make a crescent shape. Put onto the prepared trays.

4 Bake the biscuits for 20 minutes or until firm. Dust to coat in the extra dextrose while still warm. Transfer to a wire rack to cool. These are best eaten on the day they are made.

GRAVEYARD HALLOWEEN CAKES

MAKES 12

90g unsalted butter, chopped and softened

200g dextrose

1 teaspoon vanilla essence, or to taste

3 eggs

225g self-raising flour, sifted

40g cocoa powder, sifted

185ml milk

Chocolate fudge icing

200g dextrose

60g cocoa powder, sifted

100g unsalted butter, chopped and softened

125ml milk

1 tablespoon vanilla essence, or to taste

The kids will love decorating these cakes with 'dirt' (chocolate cake crumbs) and novelty Halloween items! If trick-or-treating has become a tradition in your neighbourhood and you don't want to hand out sweets, make these instead.

1 Preheat the oven to 180°C (160°C fan-assisted). Line a 12-hole muffin tin with paper cases.

2 Beat the butter, dextrose and vanilla with an electric mixer until light and creamy. Add one egg at a time, beating well after adding each one.

3 Add the flour, cocoa and milk and continue to beat until just combined. Spoon the batter evenly into the prepared paper cases.

4 Bake the cakes for 25-30 minutes or until cooked when tested with a skewer. Transfer to a wire rack to cool completely.

5 Use a tablespoon to scoop out the centre of each cupcake, leaving a 1cm border. Pulse the scooped-out cake in a food processor to form small crumbs. Set aside.

6 To make the icing, beat the dextrose, cocoa and butter with an electric mixer for 2 minutes. Add the milk and vanilla and continue to beat for 3-5 minutes or until the mixture is light and fluffy.

7 Spread a little of the chocolate fudge icing in the scooped out centre of each cupcake. Decorate with cake crumbs and Halloween items, if desired. These are best eaten on the day they are made.

GINGERBREAD

MAKES ABOUT 24

300g plain flour

2 teaspoons ground ginger

1 teaspoon ground cinnamon

½ teaspoon ground nutmeg

¼ teaspoon baking powder

110g unsalted butter, chopped
  and softened

70g dextrose

120ml glucose syrup

1 egg

1 quantity Egg-white Icing
  (see page 192)

- - - - - - - - - - - - - - - - - - - -

VARIATION:

If you wish to use these to
decorate your Christmas tree,
use a 1cm piping nozzle to
make a hole in the top of
each piece of dough before
the biscuits are baked. Run
a skewer around each hole
just after the biscuits come
out of the oven to ensure it
has a smooth edge for
threading. Thread onto your
choice of festive ribbons.

Wrapped in cellophane, these beautifully spiced biscuits make a lovely edible Christmas gift.

1 Sift the flour, ginger, cinnamon, nutmeg and baking powder into a large bowl.

2 Beat the butter and dextrose with an electric mixer until light and creamy. Add the glucose and egg and continue to beat for 2-3 minutes. With the motor on low speed, add the flour mixture and beat until the dough just comes together. Gently press together to form a disc, then wrap in plastic film and refrigerate for 30 minutes.

3 Preheat the oven to 180°C (160°C fan-assisted). Line 2 baking trays with baking paper.

4 Divide the dough in half. Place one half at a time in between 2 sheets of baking paper and roll until 3mm thick. Put each piece of dough into the freezer for 10 minutes. Use a gingerbread man, angel, star or other Christmas-themed cookie cutter to cut out shapes. Place the shapes on the prepared baking trays.

5 Bake the biscuits for 10-12 minutes or until golden. Leave to cool completely on the trays.

6 Put the icing into a piping bag fitted with a 5mm nozzle, then ice the biscuits as desired. Set aside for 2 hours or until the icing has set. Store leftover gingerbread in an airtight container for up to 2 days.

CHRISTMAS SUMMER PUDDING

SERVES 6

250g strawberries

250g raspberries

250g blueberries

70g dextrose

1 teaspoon vanilla extract,
   or to taste

60ml water

olive oil spray, for greasing

8 slices wholemeal bread,
   crusts removed

mixed berries (optional) and
   Custard (see page 192),
   to serve

A traditional Christmas pudding isn't quite the same without the dried fruit, so if a steamed pudding is what you're after try adding ground ginger to the toffee puddings on page 114. Alternatively, I like this quick, light and refreshing chilled pudding. Add a splash of brandy to the custard, if you like, to make it even more festive.

1   Put the strawberries, raspberries, blueberries, dextrose, vanilla and water into a medium saucepan. Cook, stirring frequently, over medium heat for 3–4 minutes or until the dextrose has dissolved. Strain over a bowl, reserving the liquid.

2   Lightly spray a 1 litre-capacity pudding bowl with olive oil.

3   Cut the bread slices in half, then dip 12 pieces into the reserved liquid and use to line the base and side of the pudding bowl. Spoon the berry mixture into the centre of the bowl. Dip the remaining 4 bread pieces into the remaining liquid and cover the top of the berries. Wrap the pudding bowl tightly with plastic film, then weight down with a couple of tins of food and refrigerate overnight.

4   Carefully turn out the pudding from the bowl and serve with extra berries and custard, if desired.

CHRISTMAS CUPCAKES

MAKES 12

120g unsalted butter, chopped
and softened
135g dextrose
2 eggs
1 teaspoon vanilla essence,
or to taste
300g self-raising flour, sifted
250ml milk

Hard icing
135g dextrose
1 egg white
1 tablespoon warm water

You could leave half the icing white and colour half green or red, then use the white icing to create snowflake or other Christmas-themed patterns on the top of these moist little cakes.

1 Preheat the oven to 180°C (160°C fan-assisted). Line a 12-hole muffin tin with paper cases.

2 Beat the butter and dextrose with an electric mixer until light and creamy. Add the eggs and vanilla and continue to beat until well combined. With the motor running, alternately add the flour and milk and beat until just combined. Spoon the batter evenly into the paper cases.

3 Bake the cakes for 15–20 minutes or until cooked when tested with a skewer. Transfer to a wire rack to cool completely.

4 To make the hard icing, whisk together the dextrose, egg white and water until smooth. Spread onto the cooled cupcakes. Set aside for 2 hours or until hard.

5 Serve decorated with Christmas-themed decorations, if desired. Store leftover cakes individually wrapped in plastic film or freezer bags in an airtight container in the freezer for up to 2 weeks.

ANGEL COOKIES

MAKES ABOUT 22

250g unsalted butter, chopped and
softened

135g dextrose, plus extra
for dusting

1 egg yolk

2 teaspoons vanilla essence,
or to taste

300g plain flour, sifted

Thread these pretty cookies onto ribbon and use to
decorate your Christmas tree.

1   Beat the butter and dextrose with an electric mixer for
8-10 minutes or until light and creamy. Add the egg yolk
and vanilla and beat to combine. Add the flour and beat
until a smooth dough forms. Gently press together to form
a disc, then wrap in plastic film and refrigerate for 30 minutes.

2   Preheat the oven to 180°C (160°C fan-assisted). Line 2 baking
trays with baking paper.

3   Roll out the dough between 2 sheets of baking paper until
5mm thick. Use a 7cm angel cookie cutter to cut out cookies
and place on the prepared trays. Use a 1cm piping nozzle to
make a hole in the top of each cookie (the hole for hanging
needs to be made before the biscuits are baked). Place the
dough on the prepared baking trays.

4   Bake the biscuits for 8-10 minutes or until golden. Run a skewer
around each hole just after the biscuits have come out of the
oven to ensure it has a smooth edge for threading. Leave to
cool for 10 minutes on the trays. Sprinkle with extra dextrose.
Transfer to wire racks and leave to cool completely. Store in
an airtight container for up to 5 days.

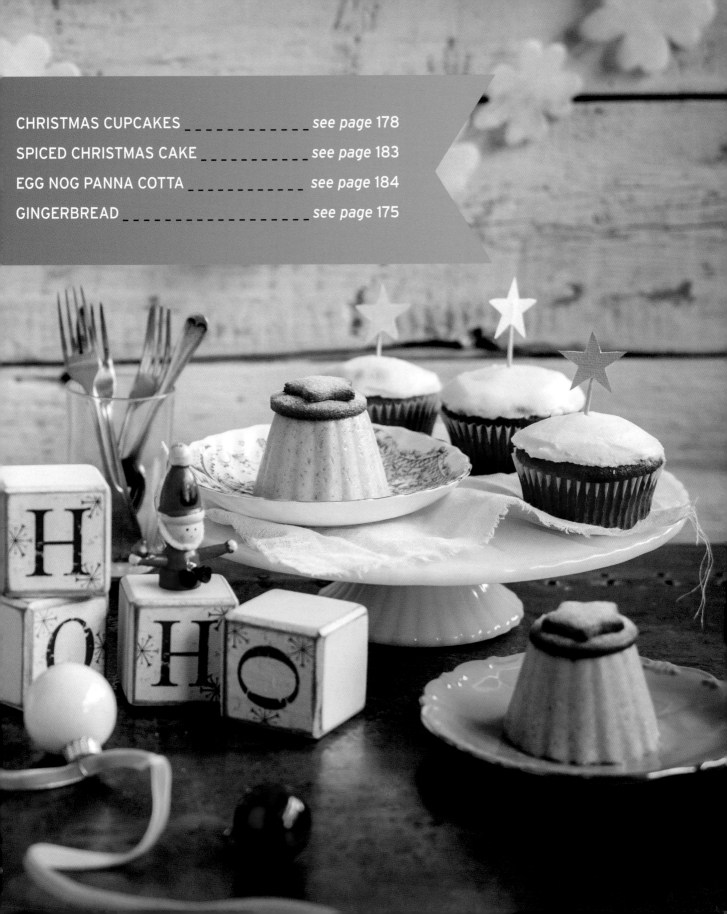

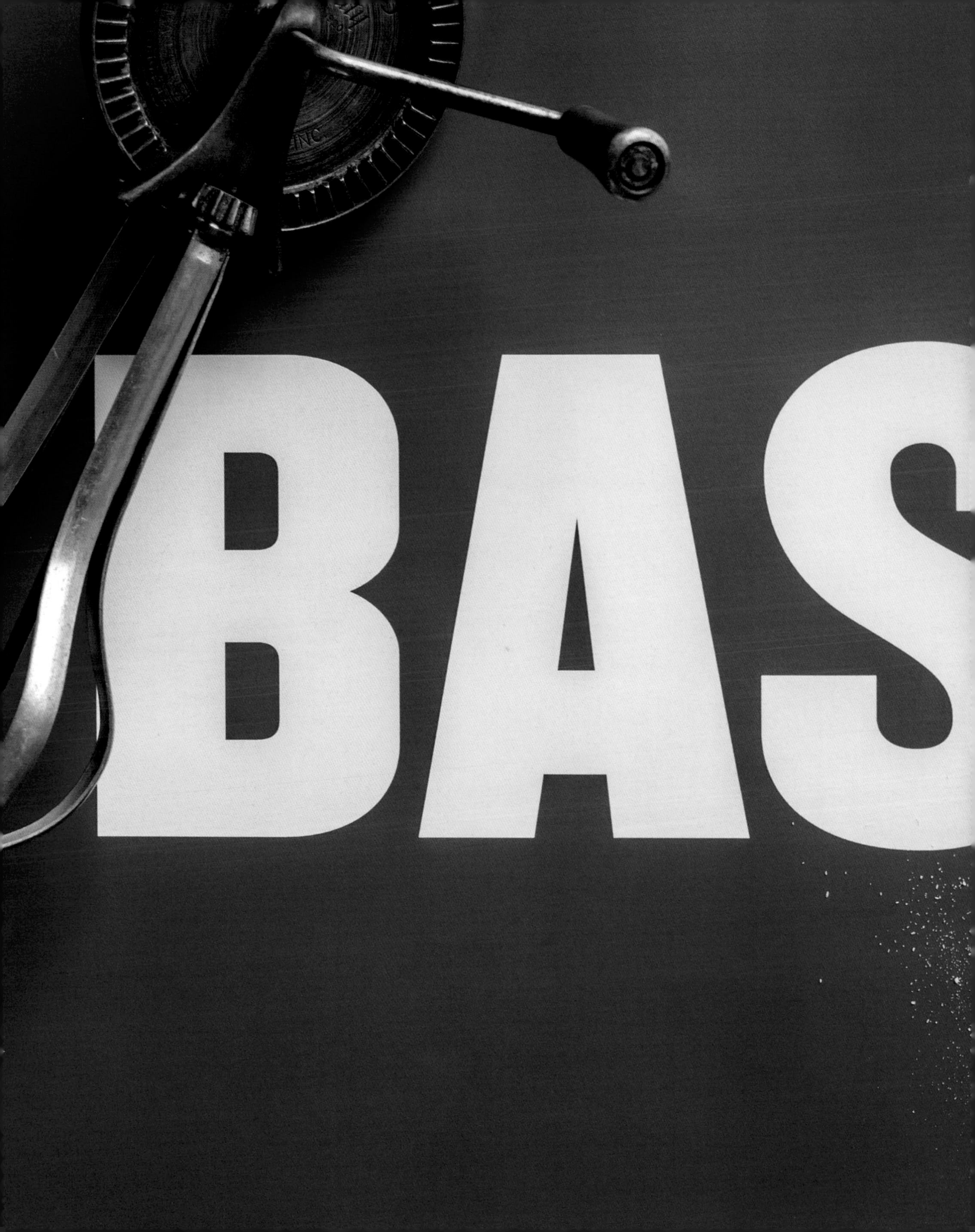
BAS

ICS

ROASTED STRAWBERRY & RHUBARB JAM

MAKES ABOUT 3 JARS

500g strawberries, hulled
and quartered

500g rhubarb stalks,
roughly chopped

2 teaspoons vanilla essence,
or to taste

270g dextrose

1 tablespoon lemon juice

This easy jam will really thicken as it cools in the fridge. It's great spread on pancakes (see page 8), scones (see page 15) or coconut bread (see page 16).

1 Preheat the oven to 180°C (160°C fan-assisted).

2 Mix the strawberries, rhubarb, vanilla, dextrose and lemon juice in a bowl until combined. Transfer to a baking dish and cover tightly with foil. Roast for 30 minutes, then remove the foil and roast for another 20-30 minutes or until thickened. Transfer to sterilised jars (see below) and leave to cool completely. Store in the fridge for up to 1 week.

- - - - - - - - - - - - - - - - - -

» TIP:

To lengthen the shelf life of your jam it is important to sterilise the storage jars. Preheat the oven to 110°C (90°C fan-assisted). Put the clean jars and lids into a deep saucepan and cover with water. Boil for 10 minutes. Carefully transfer to a baking tray lined with a clean tea towel and heat in the oven for 15 minutes.

HOT CHOCOLATE FUDGE SAUCE

MAKES ABOUT 175ML

30g unsalted butter
2 tablespoons cocoa powder
45g dextrose
125ml double cream
1 teaspoon vanilla essence,
    or to taste

1 Put the butter, cocoa, dextrose, cream and vanilla into a heatproof bowl over a saucepan of simmering water, making sure the bottom of the bowl doesn't touch the water. Heat until melted and well combined. Refrigerate for 30 minutes or until thickened slightly. Heat gently in a small saucepan over low heat, then serve warm.

ALMOND BRITTLE

135g dextrose
60g blanched almonds

1 Put the dextrose into a large non-stick frying pan and cook over medium heat for 4-5 minutes or until melted and golden. Pour onto a baking tray lined with baking paper, sprinkle over the almonds and leave to cool for 10 minutes or until crisp. Break into large pieces. Store in an airtight container for up to 3 days.

CUSTARD

SERVES 4

250ml milk
250ml double cream
1 vanilla bean, split and seeds scraped
5 egg yolks
135g dextrose

1 Put the milk, cream and vanilla into a medium saucepan. Bring just to the boil over medium heat.

2 Whisk the egg yolks and dextrose in a medium bowl until thick and pale. Gradually whisk in the milk mixture until well combined. Transfer to a clean saucepan and cook over medium heat, stirring for 4-6 minutes or until thickened. Strain the mixture through a fine-mesh sieve and serve warm or cold.

» VARIATION:
Add a little brandy to serve with your Christmas cake or pudding.

EGG-WHITE ICING

MAKES ENOUGH TO ICE 12 CUPCAKES OR 24 BISCUITS

135g dextrose
2 egg whites
1 tablespoon warm water

1 Whisk together the dextrose, egg whites and water until smooth. Use to decorate your cake/s or biscuits.

POACHED CHERRIES

MAKES ABOUT 750ML

135g dextrose
250ml water
400g cherries, stems removed, pitted

1 Put the dextrose and water into a small saucepan. Stir over medium heat until the dextrose has dissolved. Add the cherries and simmer for 5 minutes or until the syrup has thickened slightly but the cherries still hold their shape. Set aside to cool. Store in an airtight container in the fridge for up to 3 days.

ACKNOWLEDGEMENTS

Gosh it's easy to write a cookbook. Well, it's easy if your primary role is 'quality control', and all the actual work is done by seasoned professionals and your slave-driven wife. My name is on the front cover, but this book is definitely a collaboration of the very best in the business. Because I did practically nothing (other than eat pudding on a regular basis), all the author proceeds from the sale of this book are being donated to charity. My agent, Frank Stranges (who did even less than me) is also generously donating his share of the proceeds.

Peta Dent is a chef, and was responsible for designing, testing and retesting the recipes in this book. She brings an enormous wealth of cooking knowledge to the table (or should that be oven?). And besides being a consummate professional, she was an absolute delight to work with.

Vanessa Austin is the stylist responsible for making everything look gorgeous. Unlike our kids, she can make a messy spoon look like art, and she has an impeccable eye for choosing exactly the right plate to go with every single recipe. She also served as our full-sugar guinea pig at the photo shoot. Her died-in-the-wool sweet tooth meant we could get an accurate feel for how your average sugar addict would react to these dextrose-based recipes. And since a major point of this book is to give you something to feed to guests, it was important to know they wouldn't turn their noses up at any of the sweet offerings here.

Ben Dearnley clicked the button after Vanessa did the work. Not exactly, but that's how the story went at the shoot. Ben has turned out truly edible photographs. It's incredible that he can convey how the food will taste in a medium that doesn't let you smell it. I've tried, and failed, to make food look as good as Ben has managed to.

My visionary publisher, Julie Gibbs, commissioned the book – thanks Julie for continuing to champion my message. Katrina O'Brien had to find creative ways to post lamingtons and cakes across the country and deliver something that our kids were prepared to 'test', as well as making sure we delivered a book you could actually use. Kathleen Gandy edited the book and had to juggle endless alterations to the recipes with layouts, colours and extra notes about how safe some ingredients are or aren't. Emily O'Neill gave us a beautiful, playful design that makes the food jump off the page. And they all did it with grace and efficiency.

She's not on the payroll, but my wife, Lizzie, deserves special acknowledgement. Some of the recipes were developed entirely by her over years of trial and error (which was necessary because her husband banned half the contents of the supermarket). But even with the recipes developed by Peta, Lizzie has paid fanatical attention to detail. It was not good enough to just read and check – she has personally cooked most of Peta's recipes. This is the only way she can be certain they will pass the 'anyone can do this at home' test. Her devotion to the task has been truly phenomenal.

Kids will eat this stuff and love it. The only reason I can say that with absolute certainty is that all six of our munchkins (Anthony, James, Gwen, Adam, Elizabeth and Fin) have been devoted testers of chocolate cake, ice cream and all the rest. Children eating the scrumptious foods created from these pages can thank our kids for their diligence.

I hope you enjoy cooking and sharing the recipes as much as we have.

INDEX